THE MILLER'S TALE

THE
Miller's
TALE

AN AUTOBIOGRAPHY

WILLIE MILLER

with

Alastair Macdonald

MAINSTREAM
PUBLISHING

This book is dedicated to all members of my family and the many friends football has brought me, but most of all to my wife Claire, daughter Victoria and son Mark.

Willie Miller

Copyright © Willie Miller and Alastair Macdonald, 1989

First published in Great Britain in 1989 by
MAINSTREAM PUBLISHING COMPANY (EDINBURGH) LTD
7 Albany Street, Edinburgh EH1 3UG

ISBN 1 85158 155 3 (cloth)

British Library Cataloguing in Publication Data
Miller, Willie
     The Miller's Tale: an autobiography.
     1. Scotland. Association Football—Biographies
     I. Title   II. Macdonald, Alastair, *1930-*
     796.334′092′4

ISBN 1-85158-155-3

Typeset in 11½pt Imprint by Bookworm Typesetting Ltd., Edinburgh.
Printed in Great Britain by Billing and Sons Ltd., Worcester.

CONTENTS

FOREWORD

by Alex Ferguson

TO BE asked to provide a foreword to Willie Miller's autobiography is a privilege I shall cherish always. I only hope I can do it justice. Having managed him during his rise to the top, I am now in the different position of being able to view his career more objectively, but I still feel passionately about a man who has become a legend of Aberdeen Football Club.

It is a matter of personal opinion how Willie rates among Scottish football "greats" over the past 20 years, but I'm sure that as an influential club captain he would be ranked by the supporters alongside giants such as Billy McNeill, John Greig and Pat Stanton. I once said Willie was the finest player I had ever managed and now, three years on, I would not retract a word of that and I can't pay him a higher tribute than to pair him with Bryan Robson as possessors of the various attributes which go to make a great player.

This book outlines the long, hard struggle Willie has had to convince everyone in Scotland of his worth as it wasn't until after Aberdeen had won the Premier Division title in 1980 that his ability as Scotland's best defender was fully appreciated. When I had earlier tried to persuade the late, great Jock

Stein to give Willie his international chance, I was told by the Big Man that it would be easier if Willie was in a successful team. True to his word, Jock picked Willie immediately after the League success and then came the fulfilment of his great promise.

Looking back on those days, I think we may have allowed ourselves to get carried away with Willie's deeds – and why not? Didn't we all feel safe and secure if he was out there? Didn't we think that anything was possible with that Miller fire on the field? Celtic Park or Ibrox: who the hell cared? Miller was out there and that was all that mattered.

Celtic and Rangers have always been the barometer of Scottish football purely because of their great traditions, but I sincerely believe that there was a period when the Old Firm pair's players were in awe of Willie Miller, and that in itself is a testimonial to his ability.

Willie would be the first to agree with me that he also had luck on his side, which we all need. He avoided any serious injury problems, his health and family life were good, aspects which all contribute, and in addition, he had some marvellous players about him – Jim Leighton, Stuart Kennedy, his big partner Alex McLeish and others. They all helped each other and deservedly shared in the success.

For almost a decade, Dick Donald and his fellow-directors, the managers and staff, and, above all, the Aberdeen supporters have had a team of whom they could be proud, with some of the best Scottish players of their time in it. For almost two decades, they have had Willie Miller, of whom they can be doubly proud!

INTRODUCTION

by Alastair Macdonald

WILLIE MILLER and controversy are no strangers to each other. They have, in fact, been more than nodding acquaintances over the 18 years of Willie's association with Aberdeen Football Club, but more especially in recent years. Why this should be the case is a matter of conjecture, although Willie himself puts forward a possible theory when he observes that he now appears to have become the principal target for opposing fans' abuse, a burden formerly borne by Alex Ferguson when he was the Dons' manager.

In common with many top sportsmen, Willie presents two very different faces on and off the football field. In everyday clothes, quiet, reserved and one who likes to keep his own counsel, but invariably courteous, he dons a more assertive and authoritative personality along with his soccer strip. Which of these faces is the real Willie Miller it is difficult, if not impossible, to tell, but each has, at one time or another, involved him in controversy – springing in some cases from dogged reluctance to relinquish a standpoint once he is convinced of its rightness, and in others from involvement in a game so total that anything less than maximum commitment cannot be countenanced.

So, too, is it in this account of his football career. Some of the observations Willie makes on the current soccer scene or the views he expresses on the game's personalities may not meet with universal agreement, but they are not put forward just in an attempt to be controversial. They are honestly held personal opinions, moulded, in most cases, with the advantage of first-hand knowledge of the subject.

Having studied Willie Miller – the player and the person – at close hand since his early days at Pittodrie, I particularly welcomed the opportunity to collaborate with him in the writing of this book. It was a rewarding, and enlightening, experience.

Writing of his first seven years as Aberdeen manager in *A Light in the North*, Alex Ferguson described Willie Miller as "the only defender I have come across in Scottish football whom I would label as truly 'great'." This, then, is that great player's story . . .

CHAPTER ONE

Early Days

LOOKING back, one of the most surprising things about my football career is that it ever got started in the first place.

Although my family – I am the oldest of five children, with two sisters and two brothers – lived in the Bridgeton area of Glasgow, which is almost in the shadow of Celtic Park, but is primarily a Rangers' supporters' stronghold, we had no real football background. I was not even a spectator in my younger days. In fact, our closest association with the game was that an uncle used to run the bingo in Dennistoun Waverley FC's social club.

I cannot remember playing football very much until nearly the end of my primary schooling, when I was about ten. Before that I was, I think, more interested in the academic side of my life at Dalmarnock Primary School and took one or two prizes. My intellect, however, seemed to dry up when I became involved in football.

It was one of the teachers at primary school, Mr Dan Wright, and his friend, a Mr Taylor, who got me interested in football, but I must have been fairly lukewarm at first because I started as a goalkeeper, which was the position usually assigned to those less interested in the game. What they say about goalkeepers being crazy must have been true in my case for when I made the school team I found our home ground was Glasgow Green where the pitches were of red blaes. You have to be a little bit mad – or very keen – to play goalkeeper on that kind of surface. I used to go home with very little left of any exposed skin and I had to lie on whichever side was less painful.

My interest in football was stimulated by the 1966 World Cup finals in England. World Cup Willie was the official mascot and a World Cup Willie tracksuit was one of my most prized possessions. An even greater boost to my football enthusiasm, however, came from a three-week trip to America with a Glasgow Primary Select. I was one of three goalkeepers in the party. In the trial which, incidentally, was played on the pitch across the road from Ibrox, my team was beaten by something like ten goals, but, as you can imagine, in a game like that I had plenty to do and so caught the selectors' attention. It was a great trip and a terrific experience for us youngsters. I thoroughly enjoyed myself and came back dead keen to get stuck into my football.

I think the change from goalkeeper to outfield player came when I moved on from primary school to John Street Senior Secondary School. I wasn't very big at primary school, but I seemed to take off and shoot up between the ages of 12 and 13. In fact, I reached my full manhood size as a 14-year-old and when I joined Aberdeen at 16 I weighed over 12 stones, which is a bit more than my present weight.

Having decided to play out of goal, I went from one extreme to the other and became a centre-forward. At about the same time I also widened my playing horizons beyond schools football, turning out for two different boys' club teams. This assured me of three games most weekends during the football season – playing for John Street School on Saturday morning, for one of the boys' club teams on Saturday afternoon, and then for the other boys' club team on the Sunday afternoon.

That may sound a hectic programme, but for someone as enthusiastic as I was about football, it seemed quite normal. It didn't, of course, leave me much spare time for other sport-

*How do you like the haircut? I line up with team-mate Ian Wilson during
the trip to America with the Glasgow Primary Schools Select.*

ing interests, but at that time football occupied my thoughts
entirely. I don't think it happens to the same extent with
modern-day youngsters, but we used to be out at every
opportunity, especially during the summer holidays, playing
football. If there were a few of us, a game would be organised,
or if I happened to be alone, it was a game of keepie-up against
the handiest wall. I suppose there was nothing else to do in the
urban environment at that time.

Most of the playing we did was in the streets, although that
carried the risk of being chased off by any patrolling police-
men. I used to think that the bobbies did this to prevent us
doing any damage to property, but there came a time when
it was impressed on me, rather forcibly, that the police might
perhaps also be thinking of our safety. On this occasion I was
knocked down by a car while playing football in the street. I
wasn't too badly hurt, but it took me a couple of days to get
over the shock. It turned out that the car had been stolen by
someone wanting to take a joy-ride.

Street football, however, also had its happy moments, such
as when Harry Hood, who was a big name with Celtic at the
time, joined in our games. He was courting, and later married,

the daughter of the owner of the public house on the corner of the street where we played, and he couldn't resist the temptation of a kick-about.

John Street was a relatively small secondary school, so it was regarded as quite an achievement when we won the Glasgow Under-14 Cup. The team remained virtually unchanged as we progressed through the various age groups, but, apart from myself, I think there were only two other members of the side who went on to become senior professional footballers – John Docherty, who played for Bury, and Tommy Brannigan, who was with Leeds United.

As I have already mentioned, in the early years at secondary school I also played for two boys' clubs – Annfield BC on Saturday afternoons and Morton BC on Sunday afternoons. Although they were different clubs, they were associated with each other in some way and many of the boys played for both.

The John Street Secondary School Under-13 team on the threshold of success in subsequent years. That's me third from the right in the back row, with, on my left, John Docherty and Tommy Brannigan, both of whom also went on to become professional footballers.

One of my team-mates at Annfield BC was Celtic's Tommy Burns although he was, I think, almost a year younger.

In time, however, I received an invitation to join Eastercraigs, an amateur club which had started only a few years earlier but which was well on its way to its present position as one of the top clubs. I had some reservations at first about joining Eastercraigs as it meant wearing a club blazer. Having to wear a John Street School blazer during the week, I didn't fancy extending the practice into the weekends too. It took some persuasion by Ian Stevenson, one of the Eastercraigs officials, to change my mind, but now I'm deeply grateful to him for doing so. Joining Eastercraigs was one of the best steps I ever took.

On reflection, I perhaps associated wearing the Eastercraigs blazer with very strict discipline, but I soon found out it wasn't like that at all. Certainly they had definite rules that had to be observed, but nothing too restrictive and the big advantage of a club like Eastercraigs was that they were successful and consequently their games, and the tournaments they staged, attracted senior club scouts, although at the age of 13 I had no thoughts of a professional career. All I wanted to do was to play football and enjoy myself.

It wasn't too long, however, before I began to consider the possibilities of making a living from the game I loved. I'll tell you how that came about in the next chapter.

CHAPTER TWO

Aberdeen – or Celtic?

SOMETIMES, in reflective mood, I have wondered what course my life would have taken had I continued at school instead of leaving at 16 as I did. As I indicated earlier, I was quite academic at primary school and won a few prizes and for my time at John Street Secondary I earned passes in five out of the six 'O'-grades I sat, so I dare say that I could have gone on to take a few Highers. At the time, however, the question of staying on at school or not did not figure in my mind as a major decision. There was never any great choice. I was leaving school – to become a professional footballer. To this end, I had signed forms for Aberdeen when I was 14.

With hindsight, I would say without any hesitation that the decision I made was right – for me. I would, however, have to qualify that by pointing out that I have been very lucky in many ways to achieve success, and that everyone may not be as fortunate. In general, I think I would hesitate about advising a youngster to leave school as soon as he can to enter professional football if he also had the chance to go on to gain further academic qualifications. Any footballing talent he possessed would not necessarily be diluted by the extra time

Veteran chief scout Bobby Calder joins up with Joe Harper in the celebrations which followed the Dons winning the Premier Division title in 1980. Sadly, Bobby died in December, 1983.

spent at school and he would be giving himself further options when he did leave.

There I was then, a parcel in the veritable production line of youthful prospects guided towards Aberdeen Football Club by their active scouting team in the West of Scotland, headed at that time by the legendary Bobby Calder and including the club's present chief scout, Jimmy Carswell. Both those shrewd operators were involved in me joining the Pittodrie club – Jimmy in spotting me and Bobby, with his silver tongue, in persuading my mother (my parents had separated by this time) that Aberdeen was the right club for her eldest son.

That, I suppose, was fairly typical of the way Jimmy and Bobby worked together. Jimmy would do the spadework in spotting the raw talent, while Bobby, acting on Jimmy's recommendation, would watch the player a couple of times, then follow up by visiting the youngster's parents to reassure them that their son would be well looked after at Pittodrie and generally to convince them that he should sign for Aberdeen.

The oft-painted picture of Bobby is of him arriving at a young prospect's home bearing gifts – cigarettes for the father, a box of chocolates for the mother and a huge bag of sweets to dole out to brothers and sisters. While this was part of his approach, more important was his persuasiveness. Bobby was, if you like, a super salesman, selling the Aberdeen club to parents who were, in those days at least, much more concerned about how well their son was going to be looked after than in the amount of money involved. The financial aspect may figure more prominently in considerations nowadays.

Jimmy probably watched me a number of times before I was aware of an Aberdeen interest, but this interest became more obvious when Bobby became involved because he was so well known in minor football circles.

Bobby and Jimmy were a great team, producing a never-ending stream of young talent, but their work in securing my signature almost came unstuck through no fault of theirs. I was signed for Aberdeen, but my form was not registered. Apparently it was something which happened quite frequently with clubs signing more youngsters than they were permitted to register – some of the forms would lie quietly in a drawer somewhere awaiting an opportunity for registration.

It was the chap who ran the Glasgow Schools team who told me I was not registered by Aberdeen and he also asked me if I would like to talk to the Celtic scout. I agreed and I was invited to train with Celtic's 'S'-form players with a view to becoming one of their number. Thus I was faced with the choice of signing for the Parkhead club or signing for Aberdeen a second time. Although to this day I wonder why my original form was not registered by Aberdeen, I felt no resentment over their apparent neglect in failing to do so, and in the end it was my desire to get away from Glasgow which decided the issue in favour of Pittodrie – a decision I have never regretted!

I have fond memories of Glasgow in my childhood when the community spirit was really good, but by the time I was about 14 or 15 they had started moving people out to Castlemilk and Easterhouse and places like that and the whole community spirit was "out the window".

The religious divide also contributed to my feeling that I would be better away from Glasgow. It was something which never bothered me personally and I numbered both Catholics and Protestants among my friends, but I saw numerous disturbing examples of the division caused by extremists of both persuasions.

About a year after I moved to Aberdeen, the newspapers carried a front-page picture of a teenage boy who had attacked a policeman with an open razor. I could scarcely believe my eyes when I read the story for the boy concerned had gone to school with me and he was, as far as I could remember, a quite reasonable chap. Apparently, he had become involved in some group holding peculiar views on religious tolerance.

The religious issue, of course, could have its amusing side too. In Bridgeton, we lived in a tenement building where among our neighbours were a real Catholic family. There was no chance of mistaking their religion from the kind of music which frequently issued from their flat, but on the floor below there lived a family who were members of the Salvation Army, and the woman of the house did her best to drown out the Catholic music from above by hammering on her tambourine. It takes all kinds, and a Glasgow tenement certainly could provide a real cross-section of life.

When I was called up by Aberdeen in the summer of 1971, the Dons' playing staff included all the members of the squad who only a year earlier had taken the Scottish Cup to Pittodrie for only the second time in the club's history – Bobby Clark, Henning Boel, George Murray, Jim Hermiston, Tommy McMillan, Martin Buchan, Derek "Cup-tie" McKay, Dave Robb, Jim Forrest, Joe Harper, Arthur Graham and George Buchan – as well as players such as Steve Murray and Alex Willoughby. It was impressive company for a 16-year-old, even if he was starting as no more than a general dogsbody on the ground staff. A similar ground staff system still operates, but they seem to have four or five times as many youngsters going about the ground nowadays sharing the workload that I had to carry out myself, although I dare say Teddy Scott would dispute that.

As far as my playing career was concerned, however, I had nothing to complain about. After a couple of substitute appearances for the reserve team, one in a pre-season friendly at Keith and the other in a Reserve League Cup game at home to Clyde 'A', I was farmed out to Peterhead for the remainder of the 1971-72 season. The farming-out system was one I thoroughly approved of. There were not in those days so many games for those who were not in the Pittodrie reserve team and with Peterhead I was getting regular first-team football at senior level.

I went to Recreation Park as a raw youngster but I did not find playing in the Highland League as frightening an experience as I had been led to believe it might be. It used to be said that new recruits at Pittodrie were farmed out to a Highland League club to toughen them up and not all the players sent there escaped unscathed. It did me no harm at all. I was quite a physical player myself.

I remember one occasion when I, quite literally, came up against former Aberdeen goalkeeper Tubby Ogston, who was then playing, if I remember correctly, for Huntly. We went up together for a corner kick and I barged into him as he took the ball cleanly, but as we fell together I received a sharp dig in the ribs which fairly took the wind out of me. This was the experienced pro telling the young boy that he had overstepped the mark.

In addition to this lesson in what was not permissible when challenging a goalkeeper, my spell with Peterhead warned me off taking anything strong to drink on the eve of a game. Peterhead were due to travel to Buckie for a New Year's Day game, but as it seemed certain that the match would be called off because there had been a widespread snowfall, I joined in the Hogmanay celebrations rather too enthusiastically. Imagine my horror when a phone call next morning indicated that the game was on, Buckie apparently being just about the only place in the country with a pitch that was playable.

Such was my hangover that it felt as if I were having a heart attack every time I started to run. I can honestly say that that

John "Tubby" Ogston, former Aberdeen goalkeeper who taught me a valuable lesson when I was playing for Peterhead.

21

was the only professional game I played after having had a drink the night before, and it was an experience I would never wish to repeat. As such, however, it was a valuable lesson early in my football career.

As a striker, which I still was at that stage, my enjoyment of the spell at Recreation Park was increased by scoring regularly. Looking back now, I realise that those goals came from me always being involved in the goalmouth action, bustling about, rather than from any particular scoring skill I possessed. Nevertheless I finished the season with 23 goals to be Peterhead's top scorer and second top in the Highland League as a whole.

Scoring apart, I really enjoyed my season with the Buchan club, helping them win the Aberdeenshire Cup, making a lot of friends in Peterhead, and gaining valuable playing experience. At that time Peterhead were run by a three-man committee and Andy Kerr (another Aberdeen player farmed out at the same time) and I found that this system operated to our financial advantage. Although we were being paid by Aberdeen, we shared in any winning bonuses paid by the Peterhead club. When it came to paying out these £2-per-player bonuses, each member of the committee seemed to regard himself as a paymaster and consequently we received £2 from each of the three committee-men. As this just about doubled the spending money we received from Aberdeen after our digs had been paid and a proportion of our wages had been sent home, we were quite happy to accept bonuses in triplicate.

CHAPTER THREE

Down – and Up Again!

AFTER that successful season with Peterhead, in which I felt I was definitely getting somewhere in my football career, I was brought back to earth with a bump when I returned to Pittodrie for the 1972-73 season. The goals which had seemed to come so easily at Peterhead simply dried up when I donned the number nine shirt for the young Dons. Well, not entirely – I managed to score five times in the 13 appearances I made for Aberdeen 'A' in the first four months of the season. Possibly it was nothing more serious than one of those periodic lean spells which descend on every goalscorer, but to me, as a 17-year-old puffed up by my Highland League success, it appeared a disaster of major proportions. My spirits were just about as low as they could be, or so it seemed, when a big break came my way.

Saturday, 16 December was indeed a red letter day for me; one of those rare days producing a change whose influence is fully appreciated only on looking back from the vantage point of many years later. I must confess I was not altogether clear about the combination of circumstances which brought about this far-reaching change, but Aberdeen reserve team coach Teddy Scott, that never-failing authority on Pittodrie events of the past three decades, was able to fill in the details. In this case, Teddy was a particularly appropriate person to consult for he played a key role in that day's proceedings.

The date, as I said, was 16 December 1972, and Rangers 'A' were visiting Pittodrie for a Reserve League fixture. I wasn't even included in the young Dons' squad, but a couple of hours before the kick-off Teddy had a phone call to say that Ian Hair, who for the first part of the season had been playing alongside Tommy Wilson in central defence, had to call off due to sickness. Let Teddy take up the tale in his own words:

> "With the manager Jimmy Bonthrone away with the first team, I had to find a replacement for Ian Hair at very short notice and of the few players I had available, I thought Willie Miller would be the most suitable as a stop-gap defender.
>
> "Just before this Tommy Wilson had been promoted to the first team so Ian's withdrawal left me without both regular central defenders. After getting the manager's approval for my plans, I switched Billy Williamson from right-back to join Willie in the middle.
>
> "I remember my pre-match advice to Willie: 'Mark tight and try to win the ball early. Don't try anything too fancy, but if you get the chance, try to use the ball to advantage.' As things turned out Willie played that day as if he had always been a defender and we beat Rangers Reserves 2-0."

It was a touch of coincidence that it was Ian Hair, a particular mate of mine, who should be the one whose withdrawal gave me my chance as a defender, for he, like myself, had come to Pittodrie as a forward and been successfully converted into a defender. For the rest of that season I wore the number five jersey in the reserve team, with Billy Williamson as number six for a few games, and then I was joined by Ian, who was promoted in the following season to become the regular right-back choice in the first team.

It immediately became obvious to me that central defence was my true position. I realised that at that standard of football I could perform much better than I could hope to do as a striker. I hadn't, however, lost the desire to score goals and

Ian Hair, now a successful businessman, and I relax in front of the "digs" we shared as young lads on the Pittodrie staff.

managed to push my season's tally up to nine with four goals in the remaining reserve games.

At the same time, I was "chapping on the door" for a first-team place and was being tried out in practice games in full-back or midfield positions with a view to giving me occasional experience of the first team where competition for central defence was particularly keen, the established central defenders including Willie Young, Henning Boel, Tommy Wilson and George Murray.

Teddy Scott was, of course, a major influence on my early career, as he still is with youngsters arriving at Pittodrie, while George Murray was another who helped me greatly when he was appointed assistant to manager Jimmy Bonthrone. George devoted many an afternoon to working on every aspect of my game from basic things such as kicking the ball properly with either foot to more specialised defensive skills such as winning and heading clear high balls. As a defender himself, he was particularly well qualified to pass on advice about my new-found playing role.

Apart from opening up for me an entirely new aspect of football, the 1972-73 season also provided my first taste of success with Aberdeen, the young Dons completing a double in winning the Reserve League title and the Reserve League Cup. We also went to the semi-final of the Second XI Cup before losing to Hearts 'A' after a replay.

Even if I say it myself, that was a strong reserve team. Most of its members went on to become first-team regulars within a season or two. With Andy Geoghegan in goal; Billy Williamson, Chic McLelland, Ian Hair and myself in defence; Joe Smith, Jimmy Miller and John Craig in midfield; and Bertie Miller, Bobby Street, Duncan Davidson, Ian Taylor and Ian Purdie to pick from up front, it wasn't a bad side.

In addition to the success of the reserve team, I was encouraged by the indications that I was being considered as promotion material and, in fact, I had made my competitive debut in the first team before the end of that season. That was in the final League fixture of the season against Morton at Cappielow when I was substituted for Arthur Graham shortly after the interval and played up front with Barry Mitchell. We went into that game a point behind Dundee in the fight for fourth place in the final First Division table and qualification for the following season's UEFA Cup. Our 2-1 win at Greenock, combined with Dundee's 2-2 home draw against Hearts, left us level on points, but we took fourth place thanks to a two-goal advantage. Eventually, however, the complicated calculation of goal differences proved academic as Scotland's allocation of UEFA Cup places was increased to three clubs and Dundee joined Aberdeen and Hibs in the 1973-74 European tournament, with Celtic in the Champions' Cup and Rangers in the Cup-Winners' Cup.

For me personally, the big significance of the Greenock game was the remarkable transformation which it marked in my footballing fortunes – from struggling to get a place in the Aberdeen reserve team in December to making my First Division debut five months later in April. Having made that first-team breakthrough, I could hardly wait for the next season to start. Once again, though, the speed of my promotion surprised even me.

Willie Young and Henning Boel resumed their central defensive partnership in the pre-season friendlies, but the big Danish international suffered a recurrence of cartilage trouble in the opening League game against Motherwell at Pittodrie and I wore the number six shirt when we met Dundee United at Tannadice four days later. I kept it for the remainder of the season, apart from three isolated games.

When Henning returned after a knee operation, he had a spell of seven successive appearances at right-back around the Christmas and New Year period, but was subsequently released to emigrate to the United States. So my first-team career was launched on a path which, at the time of writing, sees me just over the 900 mark in appearances. For all my enthusiasm and self-confidence at that time, however, I could not have visualised what the year ahead had in store for me and the team-mates who arrived and departed around me.

CHAPTER FOUR

Opening Eyes

ONE of the least attractive aspects of professional football in my view is the frequency with which managers change jobs. I realise that the managerial merry-go-round is an inescapable fact of football life, but it is one which has caused me periodic vexation over the years. I have always had to prove myself all over again to each successive manager I have been involved with.

I don't quite know why, but many, indeed most, of the managers under whose control I have come, whether at club or international level, have started off with not too high an opinion of me or my ability and have required convincing that I'm worthy of a place in their team. Alex Ferguson, for instance, was quite frank about it and wrote in his book *A Light in the North*: "I must admit my early start with Willie Miller was not encouraging at all." I also know for a fact that Billy McNeill did not rate me very highly at first.

I have often tried to analyse this curious antipathy and have come to the conclusion that there could be a variety of causes which, either singly or in combination, could be responsible.

Some managers may have been put off by my attitude towards training. I have never been what is known as a

The first managerial team I experienced at Pittodrie, manager Eddie Turnbull and coach Jimmy Bonthrone, watch a game intently from the dugout.

"good trainer". Rather I regard preparation for a game as a necessary evil and not something to be entered into joyously. Judging solely on my training, a stranger might well get the wrong impression until he has seen me involved in a game.

Then there is my natural disposition off the field. Most of the time, I'm a quiet, rather introspective person and this might, at first acquaintance, give a mistaken impression of dourness. I think, too, that many managers are looking for elegance in their players, and elegance is not something I could claim as a description of my playing style. Effectiveness yes, but elegance no.

So, for one or more of these reasons, or for something I haven't thought of, I have frequently had a problem in my early relationship with managers. I'll return to this theme later as I deal with my club and international managers individually but, meantime, I should perhaps explain that the problem in each case has been only temporary. In general, I have eventually enjoyed good relations with all my various bosses, forged from either mutual respect or genuine liking.

When I arrived at Pittodrie as a 16-year-old, Eddie Turnbull was manager, with Jimmy Bonthrone as coach, but I was at the club only a matter of weeks before the situation was changed. Eddie left to return to the scene of his success as a player at Easter Road and Jimmy was appointed Aberdeen manager in his stead.

Obviously, I had little first-hand experience of Eddie Turnbull before his departure to take charge of Hibs, but since signing for Aberdeen I had been taking a particularly close interest in the Dons' activities and was well aware that the club's success rate had been stepped up during his managership, with a Scottish Cup final appearance in 1967, a Scottish Cup triumph three years later and finishing as runners-up in the League race in 1970-71.

I had also heard enough about Eddie's reputation as a hard taskmaster to arrive at Pittodrie more than a little in awe of my first boss. It was soon obvious to me that the players already on the staff, although wary of the manager's wrath, had a high regard for his coaching abilities. This, I think, was reflected in the number of established players who left Aberdeen in his wake. It frequently happens that when a manager moves on after a successful term with one club, the players left behind, associating that success with the manager, feel they should also seek a change of club in case the success does not continue.

Short as the time was in which I could observe the partnership of Eddie Turnbull and Jimmy Bonthrone, I was able to appreciate how two sharply contrasting personalities could complement each other so effectively. It was the bad guy, good guy combination which they worked. The impression Eddie presented was of the dour disciplinarian, while Jimmy was the players' friend, the one they related to and would consult if they had any problems. This was no pose on Jimmy's part, adopted merely to suit his role as assistant manager, or coach, as he was known at the time. Jimmy couldn't be anything other than a natural gentleman and consequently he remained the same when he became manager.

As manager, Jimmy maintained a fairly high level of discipline, but he was never as severe as his predecessor and he believed in treating his players as fellow-adults. Unfortunately, however, one or two of the senior players tried to take advantage of Jimmy's mildness. With more help from them, his spell as manager could have brought the club more success than it did.

The most public manifestation of this came near the end of Jimmy's reign as manager in the "Willie Young incident". During an early-season League game against Dundee United at Pittodrie on 13 September 1975, we were down to ten men after Joe Smith had been sent off. With about 20 minutes to go, Billy Pirie was substituted for Willie Young, who showed his displeasure by peeling off his shirt and throwing it into the dugout as he left the field.

The manager's response to this display of indiscipline was firm and swift. Willie was transferred to Tottenham three days later while the rest of the first-team squad were in Middlesbrough for an Anglo-Scottish Cup tie.

It has been suggested that Willie's tantrum was a devious way of getting a transfer as in those days a player had very little say in what happened to him once he had signed a contract. I rather think, however, that the jersey-throwing incident was just the culmination of an unhappy period for Willie Young, who only a week earlier had been one of five Scottish players banned from international selection for misbehaviour while with the Under-23 squad in Denmark.

Willie subsequently apologised publicly for his Pittodrie behaviour but the damage had been done and he was on his way to Spurs for a £140,000 fee. At the time I felt that the manager had handled the matter in the correct way, but some of my team-mates disagreed and there was quite a heated discussion while we were in Middlesbrough. It was also suggested that I would not be the same player without Willie alongside me but this was a view I disagreed with.

Willie Young was not the only one whose future was influenced by that incident for it undoubtedly affected Jimmy Bonthrone too, and almost exactly a month later the manager resigned following a home defeat against Celtic. It was entirely his own decision and one he stuck to despite a plea from the

Pittodrie board to reconsider.

In the later part of his managership Jimmy had George Murray as his assistant and they formed a good partnership, although both possibly suffered from being promoted from within the club, Jimmy moving up from coach – a role in which he was often the players' *confidant* – to manager, and George switching to coach directly from the playing ranks.

As I mentioned earlier, several members of the Turnbull team followed the manager's example in leaving Pittodrie for new pastures, the most notable departures being those of Martin Buchan to Manchester United, Joe Harper to Everton and Steve Murray to Celtic, while later in manager Bonthrone's reign there was the enforced transfer of Willie Young. The name of Bobby Clark could have been included on the list but for a last-minute hitch in a proposed £100,000 transfer to

Ally MacLeod in characteristically ebullient mood as he shows off the Scottish League Cup which the Dons won under his leadership in November, 1976.

Stoke. The hitch proved a godsend for Aberdeen as Bobby was the cornerstone of the Aberdeen team for a number of years after that.

Jimmy Bonthrone, however, also made some notable buys during his four years in office. Two of these, which were to have a longer-term significance for the Aberdeen club than could have been anticipated at the time, were the transfers of Drew Jarvie from Airdrie in 1972 and Jocky Scott from Dundee in 1974. The pair were to return to Pittodrie as part of a new managerial team more than a decade later.

Other Bonthrone captures included Zoltan Varga, Jim Henry, Eddie Thomson, Barry Mitchell, Billy Pirie, Bertie Miller and Alex Willoughby, the last-named joining his cousin Jim Forrest at Pittodrie. These newcomers cost Aberdeen a total of some £300,000, but manager Bonthrone's "good house-keeping" was reflected in a smaller number of outgoing players bringing in £500,000.

In the wake of the relatively normal managerships of Eddie Turnbull and Jimmy Bonthrone, the brief Pittodrie reign of Ally MacLeod was certainly something different – for the club, the players and the supporters alike.

Possibly the breath of fresh air which Ally brought to blow through the corridors of Pittodrie was just what the Aberdeen club needed at that stage. Ally "lifted" everyone, infecting them with his own special brand of enthusiasm, self-belief, and, on occasion, sheer effrontery. "Hype" is, I suppose, the current popular term for much of what Ally purveyed, both with Aberdeen and subsequently when he moved on to become Scotland team manager. Ally, however, had the gift of making the extravagant pronouncement credible and the seemingly hare-brained scheme workable and his methods were, at least in the short term, effective, as was demonstrated when the Dons registered a League Cup final triumph over Celtic in 1976 for the club's first domestic trophy win since the Drybrough Cup in 1971.

That success, of course, meant a lot, but equally important to the club was Ally's contribution off the field. Along with enterprising club secretary Jim Rust, he worked hard on the public relations side, improving the club's rapport with the media and the supporters.

Training was never dull with Ally in charge, particularly when it came to the practice games in which he made up new rules as he went along. You could be attacking one goal only to find suddenly that you had been switched to the other team, and goals had different values depending on whether they were scored with the head or the feet, from outside or inside the penalty box and so on. As you can imagine, keeping a tally of the score in these games was rather a complicated business and the game invariably ended with Ally having his own version of the final score. For the true score we had to consult goalkeeper Bobby Clark, who developed a habit of keeping his own tally by making a mark with his studs on the ground behind the goal whenever a "legitimate" goal was scored. The two tallies seldom agreed.

I don't think Clarkie, who was very different from Ally in character and his approach to the game, fully approved of some of the manager's methods. They certainly did not always see eye to eye, but when Ally decided to switch the team captaincy from Clarkie to me, the official reason given was that he preferred the skipper to be an outfield player who was in a better position than the goalkeeper to influence the game and his team-mates. This was just about the time that I got married and Ally claimed that the captaincy was my wedding present from him!

In keeping with his extravagant personality, Ally's disciplinary methods could, by normal standards, be described as somewhat eccentric. The story is told of how when a couple of players misbehaved, the manager had them back at the ground for extra training. Perfectly normal punishment, you might say, but Ally decreed that the extra training session should be at dead of night, so the players were sent round the Pittodrie track in pitch darkness while the manager retired to the tunnel. The only way the players knew if they were being supervised or not would be when they heard Ally's voice every now and then telling them to stop slacking, or something equally encouraging. It might sound a bizarre form of punishment, but it served

I get to carry the ball – one of the changes which Ally made was appointing me team captain in succession to Bobby Clark.

its purpose in that thereafter the threat of a late-night visit to Pittodrie was sufficient to keep players in line.

One of the manager's characteristic gimmicks was that Joe Smith was going to be the key player through whom all Aberdeen's attacks would be routed, and the adoption of this system was openly revealed to all in one of Ally's pre-season Press briefings. His instruction to players like myself was, "Win the ball and pass it to Joe." Joe Smith certainly was a superb long-ball passer, but I found it irksome to be putting a lot of effort into tackling an opponent and then simply rolling the ball to Joe once I had it.

Fortunately, the "everything goes through Joe Smith" phase did not last too long. Ally was shrewd in knowing when to change course if one of his ideas did not work out as well as expected. I think, too, that some of his excesses were curbed by George Murray, who was still club coach and had a stabilising influence on the managerial partnership.

The gradual renewal of the Aberdeen team which we had seen under Jimmy Bonthrone was continued under his successor and among Ally MacLeod's signing coups was the return to Pittodrie of Joe Harper. Joe's transfer to Everton did not prove successful. There was even a chance of him rejoining Aberdeen in February 1974, but Eddie Turnbull was also keen to sign him for Hibs and the Dons refused to enter into an auction with the Edinburgh club. Just over two years later, however, Joe, who like Willie Young had been saddled with an international ban after the Denmark incident, moved north from Easter Road to his former home.

Stuart Kennedy, Ian Fleming and Dom Sullivan were other valuable acquisitions made by manager MacLeod, while among the youngsters he brought to Pittodrie was a certain gangling redhead by the name of Alex McLeish. More on that subject later.

Ally himself, however, did not linger long enough at Pittodrie to reap the full harvest of his contribution to team rebuilding. The fresh challenge presented by the Scotland squad left managerless midway through a World Cup qualifying campaign by the resignation of Willie Ormond in May 1977 and the prospect of leading the national side into the World Cup finals in Argentina a year later was more than Ally could resist. Giving fresh impetus to an ailing cause was, after all, his forte rather than the coaching or tactical side of managership.

Just before the official announcement of Ally's appointment as Scotland manager, we had a short end-of-season holiday in Yugoslavia. During this Ally was even bubblier than usual but he didn't let the players in on his secret until we returned to Scotland.

Ally did everything on a lavish scale and his farewell party was no exception. The players were all invited out to his house at Milltimber and we arrived to find the area decorated with garlands and streamers as for a gala. He had the last laugh on us, however, because each of us had to drink a glass of a foul concoction. It was a local Yugoslavian brew with which we had been presented during our holiday and which we had taken home with us because no one in the party could stomach it.

Ally's successor as Aberdeen manager, Billy McNeill, provided us with another contrast in style. I have heard it suggested that Billy took the Aberdeen post as a stepping-stone towards his goal of the Celtic managership, and, looking back, his subsequent career made that theory more credible. I know, however, that he enjoyed his short spell at Pittodrie and had moments later in his managerial career when he regretted leaving the Aberdeen club.

I remember hearing of Billy's appointment in rather peculiar circumstances – perched on the roof of a house. At that time, with no international commitments in the summer, I found the two-month close season tended to drag for me, so to help pass the time I took a part-time job helping a joiner friend of mine. We were working on a conversion on the roof of this house when someone passing recognised me and shouted up the news that Billy McNeill was the new Aberdeen manager. I was rather surprised by the announcement, but not, I'm glad to say, enough to be in any danger of falling from my perch.

As I've already indicated, Billy was another of the managers with whom I had to overcome an initial lack of enthusiasm about my ability, but I soon had an opportunity to appreciate his enormous personal presence. I was haggling with the club over the terms of my contract and I remember Billy putting his arm round my shoulders confidentially and taking me for a stroll round the Pittodrie running track, all the while discussing our differences. By the time we had completed the circuit I found myself agreeing to re-sign for a very small increase in wages, something like an extra fiver a week!

That was the kind of aura Billy had about him. In addition to the respect he had earned as a big-name player, he was a firm disciplinarian and had obviously picked up a lot about handling people from his Celtic Park association with Jock Stein, that master of man-management.

Like Jock, Billy would weigh a case carefully before imposing his disciplinary measures, but, having decided on the punishment, he would follow through on it with great firmness whatever the cost. An example of this was when Billy dropped both Willie Garner and Bobby Glennie for the 1977-78 New Year's Day game against Dundee United at Pittodrie for failing to observe the Hogmanay curfew. Willie's absence that day allowed Alex McLeish to make his first-team competitive debut, but that was incidental. It's unlikely that Alex would have been given that chance in such a game but for Willie's disciplinary lapse.

In Billy's single season in charge at Pittodrie, the Dons' success was limited to taking second place to Rangers in both the Scottish Cup final and the Premier Division championship race and dropping out of the League Cup, again to Rangers, at the third round, but he made significant additions to the playing staff in signing Steve Archibald from Clyde and arranging the deal which brought Gordon Strachan from Dundee in exchange for Jim Shirra.

The shortness of Billy McNeill's stay at Pittodrie was yet another demonstration of how Aberdeen managers, as well as their players, have always seemed to be greatly in demand among the big clubs. In some respects this could be regarded as a tribute to the calibre of person chosen by the Pittodrie club as player or manager in the first place, but I think it is

A consoling pat on the head from Billy McNeill after a disappointing defeat.

also a reflection of the consistency with which the Aberdeen club have maintained a real challenge to the Old Firm pair for domestic honours. Clubs looking around for people to bring them success would undoubtedly have been impressed by the ever-present Pittodrie potential.

Our next manager, Alex Ferguson, was a prime example of the magnetism which Aberdeen managers seemed to have for other clubs, but he resisted numerous attempts to lure him away from Pittodrie in an eight-year period which was of deep significance to the club – and to me as team captain.

CHAPTER FIVE

Turbulent Times

THE eight years of Alex Ferguson's reign have been described as Aberdeen's "glory years" and only time will tell if the Dons' remarkable run of success in that period can be topped, or even equalled, in the future. In some ways, however, there have been many more auspicious starts to a managership than the early stages of Fergie's association with the Pittodrie club. He came, remember, under something of a cloud, stirred up by his bitter parting with St Mirren, and any chance of the dispute being quickly forgotten was ruined by the subsequent and exhaustively publicised industrial tribunal hearing.

As far as the Aberdeen players were concerned, the new manager was a relatively unknown quantity beyond recognition of the good job he had done with limited resources at Love Street – surely an inappropriate name for the home of a club caught up in a war of words as St Mirren were at that time. In fact, the first year to 18 months of Alex Ferguson's Aberdeen managership was a turbulent period as the Pittodrie players, particularly the more senior of us, came to terms with the new boss, a man of strong personality who had very definite ideas about what he wanted and was equally definite in his determination to achieve his aims.

At that time, of course, I was still inexperienced as team skipper and I frequently consulted Bobby Clark, who was regarded as the elder statesman among the Pittodrie playing staff, for advice on how to handle this or that situation. Looking back, I now realise that most of the concern I felt arose from me not understanding fully what was going on and what Fergie was trying to do.

One of the minor personal irritations I had to endure at first was having St Mirren's Jackie Copland constantly held up as a model on which I should base my play. Every time we had a practice game, the manager would at some point remark: "Jackie Copland would have cleared that ball" or "Jackie would have done it this way". Much as I respected Jackie as an excellent player, frankly, I thought that my method of doing things was just as effective and I did not appreciate the constant comparison. In fairness to the manager, however, he soon got the message that this particular kind of comment irked me and he stopped the practice.

Nevertheless, it took some time for Alex Ferguson and me to build up the relationship of mutual respect and understanding which we finally achieved. We still had the occasional head-to-head with neither willing to give way and I remember one occasion when he replaced me for the second half of a game because I would not back down from the stand I took in an interval discussion in the dressing-room.

It was a game against Partick Thistle at Firhill, where we had been playing a system with five at the back and not making a great success of it. We probably both took the argument further than we should, with neither prepared to see the other's point of view, but, as manager, Fergie had the final word and the upshot was that I had an early bath. Strangely enough, however, this incident seemed to bring matters between us to a head and thereafter our relations steadily improved. Possibly the dressing-room "barney" had shown us just how far we could go with each other.

Fergie was a very determined character but I didn't mind that, as long as it was for the good of the club and brought success. In his case, it invariably was for the good of the club and certainly brought success. The success which came to Aberdeen under his handling was another strong argument in favour of accepting his viewpoint on how things should be done. What player in his right mind would put up more than token opposition to a manager who in the course of an eight-year reign led the club to three League, four Scottish Cup, one League Cup and two European trophy triumphs?

One interesting aspect of Alex Ferguson's managership was that while Pat Stanton, Archie Knox and Willie Garner, the three assistant managers to serve under him at Aberdeen, were all different from each other in their personal make-up, each made a contribution towards complementing the manager himself and achieving a balance in the management team.

Pat was something like Billy McNeill in that he came to Pittodrie as someone highly respected as a player. In this pairing, he was the quiet, level-headed one who balanced Fergie's fieriness and determination.

Archie was less of a contrast to the manager himself than Pat was, but the points of similarity Fergie and Archie shared had the beneficial effect of them striking sparks off each other. Archie is a first-class advertisement for the modern SFA coaching school, which has come a long way since its early days when it tended to attract only the players from the lesser clubs and was run by coaches who were stronger on theory than they were on the practical side. Now it is a well-respectd system and much of its higher profile, I feel, is due to the people who have served it as staff coaches – people such as Alex Ferguson, Archie Knox, Alex Smith, and, of course, the National Director of Coaching, Andy Roxburgh. Archie's dedication to training bordered on the fanatical and there were times when the manager had to intervene to bring a session to an end – to the great relief of the players involved, but to the annoyance of Archie.

Archie's successor as assistant manager, whoever he was, was going to have a hard act to follow, and Willie Garner was perhaps a little short on experience and possibly even in years – he is younger than I am – to bear comparison with Archie. Willie's appointment came as a surprise and equally surprising was his departure just over two years later when Archie returned to the club with the new title of co-manager but virtually the same area of responsibility as before.

Despite his relative inexperience and a tally of years which left age-gaps fairly narrow between the players and himself and consequently fairly wide between the manager and himself, Willie did a competent job and his displacement was no reflection on his coaching ability. He was just unfortunate to be caught up in an interlude in the club's life which had even the players puzzled.

In the later stages of Alex Ferguson's reign I got the feeling occasionally that he was perhaps thinking it was time to move on in his constant search for the impossible goal of absolute perfection. This brings me to one point on which I would perhaps disagree with his philosophy about keeping players.

I did not, for example, think it was a good thing when players, who might have been persuaded to stay with a little more inducement from the management, were allowed to leave the club. Fergie, however, took a different view. He felt that it was always possible to find better players and thus achieve even higher standards. That might be all right in theory, but I think that in practice – and recognising that a club like Aberdeen, while reasonably wealthy, does not have unlimited funds at its disposal – you sometimes have to accept that absolute perfection is simply not attainable.

Allowing, however, that Fergie was always striving for perfection, his decision to accept an offer from a club of Manchester United's standing was not altogether surprising. That did not lessen the sense of loss his departure brought to the Aberdeen club.

After a successful eight-year association, stormy though it may have been in the early stages, it is understandable that Alex Ferguson and I should keep in touch with each other and follow each other's career with great interest. That is why Fergie was the first person I thought of to provide a foreword for this book. I have visited Old Trafford at his invitation and been shown over United's impressive set-up and we chat on the telephone from time to time, getting up to date with each other's thoughts on current soccer topics.

When Fergie went to England I was convinced that he, if anyone, could restore Manchester United to its former place in football. I still think that way, but it will obviously take a little time to achieve that objective. Manchester United is such a big institution that it has to be handled differently from other clubs, particularly in the aspects not directly to do with football.

Fergie, too, has had rather a hard time with the English Press, partly, I suppose, because he is not the kind of manager to endear himself to tabloid journalists as his predecessor Ron Atkinson did.

I'm sure, however, that Fergie still relishes his task and I'm equally sure that he will succeed eventually. He seems to be shaping the team more to his own liking now, getting rid of some players who have perhaps been at Old Trafford for too long and bringing in new faces in their place.

Almost inevitably, Alex Ferguson's sucessor at Pittodrie was going to have a hard row to furrow and, in the event, I think there was fairly general agreement that Ian Porterfield had too much going against him to succeed in the thankless task of making everyone connected with the Pittodrie club forget about his predecessor. A wide variety of theories have been advanced as to why he failed, but I think it was a combination of factors rather than one single reason.

Ian came to Pittodrie almost unknown, at least in a football management context. The only thing most North-East people, myself included, remembered about him was that he scored the FA Cup final winning goal for Sunderland in 1973. Such anonymity need not have been an insurmountable handicap, for, after all, not too much was known about Alex Ferguson as a manager when he was appointed, but Ian's wide range of contacts in England did not fully compensate for his unfamiliarity with the Scottish soccer scene. This shortcoming might have been minimised with the appointment of a home-based assistant – no disrespect to Jimmy Mullen who subsequently came north to take up this position – with former Don Tommy Craig being one of the names mentioned.

Then there was the rather negative system of play Ian adopted which did not go down too well with Aberdeen fans who had been educated to expect three men playing up front, even if one of them was deep-lying but could be regarded as a winger.

It did not help either that Ian, a quiet, retiring person by nature, did not relate to the supporters well enough to swing them round to his way of thinking. Despite this, however, the bulk of the Dons' fans were tolerant and did not give him a hard time. Neither did the players.

His biggest misfortune in this respect came from the unfortunate publicity to which his private life was exposed. Certain newspapers, as we have all discovered, make a meal of things like that.

It all added up to an unfortunate period for the club, considering the preceding managers we had: Ally MacLeod, who had a rapport with the supporters and the media; Billy McNeill, who had great presence; and Alex Ferguson, who brought the club success in abundance. Ian Porterfield, sadly, had none of these things working for him.

It is a different story with the present Pittodrie management. The degree of success which the combination of Alex Smith, Jocky Scott and Drew Jarvie can achieve remains to be seen, but there is no doubt that the potential for success is there and this is at least partly because the management team set-up allows all its members to contribute different qualities. In this I include Teddy Scott along with the three others because Teddy fulfils a unique function at Pittodrie. Having served under no fewer than nine managers, he has built up a wealth of experience and provides a sense of continuity which few in Scottish football can match. This depth of experience, together with his unquestioned loyalty to the club and his conscientious attention to detail, are assets which successive managers have recognised and treasured. When Billy McNeill left Pittodrie for Celtic Park, it was rumoured that he wanted to take Teddy with him, while the high regard in which he was

Alex Ferguson, in charge of a training session at Aberdeen. It was a difficult act for the new manager to follow when Fergie left to manage Manchester United.

A cornerstone of the Pittodrie establishment, Teddy Scott prepares the portable goalposts for a practice game.

held by Alex Ferguson was indicated by his inclusion in the Scottish technical staff for the World Cup finals in Mexico.

The term co-manager has, in my view, a certain ambiguity but whatever titles are used, the various members of the management team should have particular spheres of responsibility, which may overlap in some areas, and the ideal is that they should work so well together that the overall product of their efforts is greater than the sum of their individual contributions.

In Aberdeen's case, we have Alex Smith as the senior partner, highly respected in the game, particularly on the coaching side – a "father figure" for want of a better term, although I'm not too sure he would altogether approve of such a description. Alex is the front man for the club in its relations with the media and he also handles negotiations with players over contracts. He sometimes takes a hand in the training, but for the most part that is Jocky Scott's domain, while the two of them hammer out the team's playing tactics between them. Drew Jarvie, whose main responsibility through the week is training the reserves, also has input in match situations for all three of them are with the first team for games, with Teddy Scott looking after the reserve-team.

In Jocky Scott and Drew Jarvie we have two former Aberdeen players who have had the advantage of spells with other clubs before returning to Pittodrie in management capacities. Alex also has a long-standing association with the club from the days when, through his friendship with Alex Ferguson, he was a regular visitor for the European ties.

As I have already said, it is a promising blend.

Reviewing the various club managers I have worked with, though, the most influential as far as I'm concerned would be, undoubtedly, Alex Ferguson. Certainly I have picked up valuable bits and pieces from my other bosses, but the combination of Fergie's Pittodrie managership being the longest I have experienced and it bringing the club its greatest success obviously puts it in a class of its own.

That's not to say that if ever I become a manager I would try to mould myself on the way Fergie managed the club.

For one thing, we are completely different personalities and that, to some extent at least, dictates how you go about the job. A lot of what I have learned from the various Aberdeen managers, particularly Fergie, could well be adapted to suit my style.

CHAPTER SIX

Thanks, Jim!

ANYONE remembering the incident involving Jim McLean and myself in the 1987-88 Scottish Cup semi-final and the hot water it subsequently got him into with the SFA would probably find it difficult to believe either the Dundee United manager or myself having a kind word to say about the other. Nevertheless, I believe I have Jim McLean to thank for helping me at a crucial stage of my international career. The occasion was a World Cup qualifying game against Israel in Tel Aviv in February 1981, with Jock Stein as Scotland manager and Jim as his assistant. The story, however, begins five months earlier when we met Sweden in Stockholm in the opening game of the qualifying series.

The night before announcing his team, Jock Stein told me I would be playing as sweeper alongside Alex McLeish, but the next morning he took me aside and said: "I've got a problem, and you're the only man that can help me out of it" – a typical approach by the Big Man when he was seeking a favour. When I asked what his problem was, he explained that he had intended playing Alex and myself in the middle of the defence with Alan Hansen in a midfield role. "That's my problem," he said. "Hansen doesn't fancy playing in midfield. Will you help out by playing there instead?"

Well, at that stage of my international career, I would have played anywhere to wear a Scotland jersey, so I agreed, although with some reluctance. I had, after all, operated as a defensive midfield player when I made my full international debut under Willie Ormond in Rumania more than five years earlier.

In the Swedish game I did well enough. Nothing outstanding, mind you, but a reasonable performance in the circumstances, although I remember getting stick from Ian St John on the television for missing a chance. No mention was made of several chances missed by other players who were more accustomed to putting the ball in the net. Perhaps the commentator knew them a bit better than he knew me and that made me an easier target.

That was in September and our 1-0 win, with Gordon Strachan scoring the all-important goal, gave us a good start to the qualifying campaign. A month later, we entertained Portugal at Hampden and, with Alex McLeish on the injured list, Alan Hansen and I formed the central defensive partnership. The game ended in a reasonably satisfactory no-scoring draw.

Then it was on to Tel Aviv in February – but this time I was only on the bench. The manager had recalled Kenny Burns to the squad, after almost a year's absence, for the Sweden game, but he had withdrawn through injury and was left out of the squad against Portugal. In Israel, however, he started the game alongside Alex McLeish, with yours truly as a substitute. Possibly my viewpoint was jaundiced by disappointment, but I thought Kenny didn't look completely fit in training, and altogether I was so disgusted by him being preferred to me that I was considering packing in international football before I had properly started in it. Even the fulfilment of my doubts about Kenny Burns' form in a first half which saw Scotland annihilated by the Israeli "no hopers" and lucky not to be three goals down at the interval, did not give me any satisfaction and I did not join the other substitutes in the half-time kickabout.

Just when my spirits were at their lowest, as I was sitting there on the subs' bench nursing my grievance, I saw Jim McLean hurrying from the dressing-room towards the bench. When he arrived, he told me that I was going on as second-half replacement for John Wark, who had pulled a hamstring, and that I would be playing as sweeper with Kenny Burns moving into midfield. My day was complete when a second-half goal by Kenny Dalglish, playing in his 78th international, gave us a victory we scarcely deserved and left us sharing top place in the group with Portugal.

I've never been able to confirm it, but I'm fairly sure that it was Jim McLean who persuaded the Big Man to make that half-time change – not that that established me as an automatic choice for the team, as some time was still to elapse before Jock was convinced that I was the best man for the number six jersey. It was, nevertheless, an important step towards that end.

Jock Stein was not an easy man to get to know, and, as with all football managers, he had his likes and dislikes among players. While my relationship with him took some time to flourish, he seemed to take an instant shine to my team-mate Alex McLeish. I used to wind up big Alex by calling him "Big Jock's boy"!

I have never been able to account for Jock Stein's apparent early antipathy towards me. It may simply have been a case of him having doubts about my ability in an international context. Although, as I have indicated elsewhere, I disagreed with Jock's view on certain defensive systems, I couldn't say it was a personality clash, for Jock had a very strong personality and few of the players were a match for him in that respect. Whatever the reason, there must have been some significance in the fact that, following Jock's appointment as Scotland manager in October 1978, I was used only once in 13 internationals in his first 20 months in office. Starting with the home championship match against Wales in May 1980, however, I missed only ten of the remaining 48 games of his reign, and captained the side five times in that period.

I was as profoundly affected as anyone by the Big Man's sudden death on that bitter-sweet night of 10 September 1985 at Ninian Park, Cardiff. Really, all I can remember about that night were contrasting emotions. From being high on the realisation that we had qualified for the World Cup finals, assuming, of course, that we could account for Australia in the extra round, we were plunged to the depths by the news that the Big Man had died. It was undoubtedly the way Jock would have wanted to go, but the sense of shock and loss was still very sharp.

Alex Ferguson's agreement to take on the Scotland manager-ship for the duration of our involvement in the World Cup finals brought me for a second time into the position of serving an international team manager who had also handled me at club level. On the earlier occasion, however, I had only limited experience of Ally MacLeod as the Scotland boss. Ally twice used me as an over-age player in the Under-21 squad, against Switzerland and Czechoslovakia, but my only full international appearance under him was in a home friendly against Bulgaria in February 1978, when I partnered Gordon McQueen in central defence in a game we won 2-1. I was also in the squad for Ally's last international, an away European championship qualifying match against Austria six days before his resignation, but I was not used even on the bench.

Actually, I came close to having more international exposure during Ally's reign as, at one stage, there seemed to be a chance of me going to the World Cup finals in Argentina. I had been included in the initial 40-strong squad and was named a stand-by when it was reduced to the 22 to travel. My prospects of being called in brightened when Gordon McQueen was injured during the home championship series just before the Scotland squad left for South America, but Ally decided to take Gordon along in the hope that he would have recovered in time for the matches. In the event, the Manchester United defender's fitness doubts persisted and the fact that he had taken a player who had only an outside chance of being fit was later used as a stick to beat Ally's back in the recriminations which followed the Argentina debacle.

I did not, however, feel any bitterness over Ally's decision to take Gordon McQueen, although it deprived me of

The Big Man in action during an international training session.

a possible chance to join Aberdeen clubmates Bobby Clark, Stuart Kennedy and Joe Harper in the World Cup squad. Taking Gordon was the kind of calculated risk any manager might have undertaken in similar circumstances and my not having played in any of the qualifying games would not have made the decision any easier for the manager.

By the time I had my second experience of working under an international manager I had known at club level, I was a seasoned professional with 40-odd caps behind me and I had captained Scotland half-a-dozen times.

During Alex Ferguson's brief Scotland reign, I was never aware of having my club manager as my international manager posing any problem for me, but I think the situation possibly produced some conflict for him. There could have been evidence of this, for example, when he left Alex McLeish out for the Uruguay game even though he seemed to have recovered from the flu bug which ruled him out of the previous game against West Germany, and could only find a place on the bench for Jim Bett. Fergie possibly felt that, as Aberdeen manager, he had not only to be impartial, but had also to be seen to be impartial.

In the context of present-day international football, the demands are such that I would say that combining the two jobs is more than anyone can safely handle. Probably the present Scotland set-up is as near ideal as you can get, with the national director of coaching doubling as team manager. The two roles seem complementary in many ways.

The appointment of Andy Roxburgh following the World Cup finals came as a surprise to just about everyone, as it broke completely with the tradition of drawing international managers from the ranks of club management. Although you would hardly expect me to express any other view, I do honestly believe that the new system is working well and that Andy Roxburgh is handling the complex demands of the manager's job efficiently.

Before leaving the subject of international managers I have been associated with, I would like to make some reference to the earliest of these – Willie Ormond.

Willie Ormond, the Scotland manager who gave me my first chance at full international level – and almost lost his job after the same game.

It was Willie who gave me my first full international cap when he promoted me from the Under-23 squad to play – in midfield – against Rumania in a European championship qualifying match in Bucharest on 1 June 1975. It was a rather makeshift side, for in addition to the earlier withdrawals of David Hay, Derek Johnstone and Martin Buchan, Leeds United players Billy Bremner and Joe Jordan, who were to have joined the squad after playing for their club against Bayern Munich in the European Cup final, were injured in the Paris game and didn't travel to Rumania. We managed, however, to escape with a 1-1 draw thanks to Gordon McQueen scoring the first of the five goals he notched up in his 30-cap international career.

That Rumanian trip was also memorable for another, very different, reason: the difficulty we had getting out of the country after the game. There was some problem with the plane coming to pick us up and we had to endure a five-hour wait in broiling heat in Bucharest Airport. To make matters worse, we had already gone through customs and the other departure procedures before news came of the flight's delay, so we were confined for the long wait to a departure lounge which eventually felt like a glass greenhouse, with mean-looking heavily armed guards keeping an eye on the party.

I was sure these gentlemen were taking a particular interest in me because during the game one of my tackles brought an end to the involvement of Rumania's star player Dude Georgescu. I was told by some of the other players that the guards had been asking them questions obviously aimed at identifying the perpetrator of this "crime" so I adopted my own version of "keeping a low profile". I withdrew to a quiet corner of the lounge and indulged in my favourite pastime by having a nap.

If the air in that departure lounge was not circulating too freely, the rumours certainly were and the frustration of the long delay helped fuel speculation that Willie Ormond was due for the chop from the Scotland job when we returned home. Judging by his air of dejection, even Willie himself seemed convinced that the rumours had some substance. When we did get back to Scotland, of course, the speculation about Willie's future was given free rein in the Press, but this seemed to set up a counter-current of sympathy for him. In fact, he remained as Scotland manager for almost two years after that.

Willie Ormond was an easy-going individual and, with so many strong characters in his squad, notably Billy Bremner and Danny McGrain, I, as a comparative youngster and newcomer, sometimes wondered who was running the show. Certainly Willie permitted his players more licence in deciding how a game was to be played than most managers would allow, but that was just his way. He picked the team, laid down a general pattern and then let his players get on with it.

CHAPTER SEVEN

The Winning Habit

SOMEONE once said that success breeds success. Expressing a similar theory, but reducing it to slightly more vulgar terms, it could be said that success is like wearing a new set of dentures: achieve it often enough and it becomes easier to achieve. This observation is prompted by the experience I have accumulated in close on two decades as a professional footballer, with particular reference to the fortunes of the Aberdeen club in domestic competitions.

When I arrived at Pittodrie in the early 70s I was joining a club still basking in a sense of achievement from their 1970 Scottish Cup triumph, but with the team who had brought the trophy north for the first time in 23 years beginning to break up. So by the time I had established myself in the first team three seasons later, we had no immediate history of success, and, indeed, had only four or five survivors of the 1970 Cup final in the side.

At that period, we tended to measure our success not in trophies won, but in whether or not we qualified for Europe, and for that a place among the top four in the old 18-club First Division was generally enough to satisfy our ambitions. This, however, left Aberdeen at a distinct disadvantage to Rangers and Celtic, both of whom had the history of success we lacked and also had in their teams a preponderance of players who were accustomed to handling the extra pressure occasioned by playing in Cup finals and League deciders. Even then, we would always fancy our chances of beating either of the Old Firm teams in a Cup-tie because of its one-off nature, but in the long, hard slog of the League competition it was a different matter.

The beginning of change coincided with the arrival in January 1976 of a new manager in Ally MacLeod, and that, I feel, was not merely coincidental. We finished the 1975-76 season – the first of the new-look Premier Division – in seventh place, avoiding relegation only on goal difference, but by the following season Ally had infected everyone connected with the club with his bubbling enthusiasm and we made the initial breakthrough by winning the League Cup.

That was in November and despite an early Scottish Cup dismissal by Dundee in a fourth-round replay at Pittodrie, the ultra-persuasive Ally had us convinced that we were going to win the League. In the event, we finished third behind Celtic and Rangers, but a full 12 points lay between us and the Parkhead club in the final table.

In fact, the 1976-77 League Cup triumph was the only indication of a change in Aberdeen's fortunes in that season but the movement, once started, began to pick up momentum under Billy McNeill in the following season when we finished as Premier Division runners-up, two points behind Rangers, our tally of 53 points being five points better than our title-winning total of 1979-80. In addition to making a genuine challenge to the Old Firm in the League, we reached the final of the Scottish Cup, but once again had to give best to Rangers.

I remember the bitterness of the disappointment everyone, including Big Billy, felt over that 2-1 Cup final defeat, particularly in contrast to the joy we had experienced in our League Cup success of the previous season, but in retrospect I realise that setbacks like that are in a way complementary to successes. They go together as essential parts of the hardening process that a team must go through on its way to full maturity.

In our case, that maturity was reached a few seasons later under Alex Ferguson. A triumphal progress through the early to mid-80s, launched by winning the Premier Division title in 1979-80, his second season in charge, and eventually extending to four Scottish Cup, one League Cup and three League honours, to say nothing of the Cup-Winners' Cup and the Super Cup in European competition, saw us cultivate the winning habit.

The winning habit is reflected not only in lifting trophies regularly, although that is its most obvious and important manifestation. It also produces beneficial side effects.

Probably the most significant of these in our case was a shift

A proud moment as I hold aloft the Premier Division trophy after receiving it from Scottish League president David Letham.

Another manifestation of the "winning habit". Team-mates Duncan Davidson, Chic McLelland, Ian Fleming, Gordon Strachan and Steve Ritchie showing a keen interest in the gallon of whisky I received as Mackinlay's Scottish Football Personality of the Month. Curly hair seems to be in fashion.

in our attitude towards Rangers and Celtic: coming to regard ourselves as the equals of the Old Firm pair much more than had been the case in earlier years. This arrogance probably contributed to our League Cup and Scottish Cup double in 1985-86, when we beat Hibs and Hearts in the respective finals, by a 3-0 margin in each case. In these games, the Edinburgh sides were cast in the role of underdogs which we would have found ourselves occupying ten years earlier had we been meeting either Rangers or Celtic.

Another respect in which we became more like the two big Glasgow clubs was in our acquisition of the knack of winning without playing at our best. An example of this was our 1-0 extra-time win over Rangers in the 1982-83 Scottish Cup final, ten days after our European triumph in Gothenburg. Most of the team were roundly slated by Fergie for their Hampden performance and although the manager made a public apology the following day, his earlier criticism was at least partially justified as we had, perhaps understandably, not been at our best in that game.

Aberdeen's emergence as a consistently successful side in the '80s could also be measured in new records for undefeated runs. Over a period spanning parts of two seasons, between February and December 1980, we played 30 League games without defeat, and equalled the Premier Division record of 17 home League games unbeaten, while during March and April of 1982 we recorded seven successive League wins in the course of a 15-game undefeated run. Another record was equalled in March 1984 when we completed a series of 27 competitive games without defeat since mid-October 1983. A season later, our record for an unbeaten run of home League games was boosted from 17 to 24 games.

Although these unbeaten runs were pointers to the team's consistency, Alex Ferguson was always at pains to ignore them in his team talks. In fact, he kept drumming into us to forget all about them, as he was aware how much added pressure they contributed. As a series progressed, you began to go out on the park with the feeling that you weren't going to lose, but as the breaking of an old record neared, speculation on how long the run could last would be taken up by the Press. It would then start preying on the players' minds, with possibly fatal consequences.

Realistically, it doesn't matter how many games you have gone without defeat, the next one is only another game, another obstacle to be overcome, but it is sometimes difficult to see things in that light after reading in newspapers that you have only so many games to go to set a new record. Fortunately, Fergie could be very persuasive in his arguments against paying attention to newspaper speculation.

I have been discussing the winning habit, but there is also a losing habit, and it is something which can afflict even an otherwise successful team. Just think of Dundee United, who have frequently in recent years gone all the way in competitions only to stumble at the final hurdle.

This problem seemed to threaten Aberdeen when, following our defeat in the 1977-78 Scottish Cup final, we suffered a similar fate in two successive appearances in the League Cup final, against Rangers in 1978-79 and Dundee United after a replay in the following season. These two reverses and our subsequent failures at earlier stages of the League Cup competition in the next five years gave credence to the idea that the competition was ill-fated as far as Fergie was concerned, a suggestion which thankfully was laid to rest when we won the Skol Cup, as the competition had by then become, in 1985-86, which turned out to be Fergie's last full season as Aberdeen manager.

Apart from the adverse psychological effect on players, the biggest danger of the losing habit is that the fans, having had their expectations for the final nourished by the pre-match publicity, become increasingly disheartened.

I remember returning from one of these League Cup final defeats and, as the coach and its load of glum footballers drew up at Pittodrie, the headlights picked out the rebuke "Dons, you've let us down again" scrawled in large letters on the main entrance grille. It had probably been some of the "idiot few" who had seized on the opportunity to go mad with an aerosol paint spray, but this particular piece of graffiti was the last message the Aberdeen party wanted to receive on top of their Hampden disappointment. It only added to the pain of losing.

CHAPTER EIGHT

The Psychology of Success

IN THE last chapter I referred briefly to the psychology of success as it has been reflected in our attitude towards Rangers and Celtic over the past decade or so. The change in attitudes which has taken place in that period, however, has not been one-sided. I believe the Old Firm clubs' attitude towards Aberdeen is even more volatile than ours to them and is very dependent on circumstances. If we are beating them consistently, as we were for a lengthy spell a few years ago, they seem to accept that gracefully enough, but it is a different story if they are on top and feel that we are likely to challenge their supremacy. Then things can get quite nasty.

I remember one outstanding example of this in Alex Ferguson's first season – 1978-79 – when we were drawn at home to Celtic in the quarter-final of the Scottish Cup. After a 1-1 draw at Pittodrie, Celtic were convinced they had the tie won and that the Parkhead replay would be little more than a formality. We surprised them, however, by winning 2-1 at Celtic Park, but what I remember most vividly about that game was the hostile atmosphere in the ground. It was so intense that it was almost tangible, and the hostility was transmitted from the huge Celtic support to their players.

When the game ended, there was a scuffle among the players in the tunnel with Bobby Clark being the innocent victim of an attack by an unknown assailant. It was no consolation to the big 'keeper that at the time he was trying to keep the peace by restraining Celtic winger Johnny Doyle from "having a go" at the referee as the teams left the pitch. In the ensuing mêlée, a flying punch caught Clarkie full on the jaw and his attacker disappeared discreetly into the Celtic dressing-room.

The whole incident was no more than a minor dust-up and it even had its amusing side, if you could overlook the pain and embarrassment, Clarkie's efforts as a mediator cost him, but, allied to the atmosphere which the game itself generated, it produced a match which was memorable for the wrong reason.

The heavy toll of bookings and sending-offs in matches between Rangers and ourselves is discussed fully elsewhere in the book, but that too is an indication of Old Firm reaction to an Aberdeen challenge for honours. There are other occasions when psychological forces outweigh factors such as the players' skill and commitment which normally decide the outcome of a football match.

Generally speaking, I don't believe in the term "bogey team", but I suppose I would have to make an exception in the case of Dundee United, considering the number of times the Tannadice side have knocked us out of cup competitions.

The worst of these dismissals from our point of view would have to be in the 1979-80 League Cup final. Having accounted for Rangers and Celtic in successive rounds, winning both home and away legs in each case, followed by a win over Morton – another possible candidate for the "bogey team" description – in the semi-final at Hampden, we were entitled to believe that we deserved to win the competition. So we should have, for against United in the Hampden final we had a couple of scoring chances and had what we considered a stone wall penalty claim turned down late in the game when substitute Drew Jarvie was brought down by former Don Steve Murray.

The tie, however, finished in a no-scoring draw and when

we went to Dens Park for the replay four days later, we were simply torn apart – there's no other way to describe it – in a 3-0 defeat. Losing three goals in a game was in itself a rare occurrence for us, and to this day I cannot think of any good reason why we should have lost that one as we did, apart from the fact that Paul Sturrock had a very good game for United on that occasion.

It is not only in cup-ties that Dundee United have inflicted crucial defeats on Aberdeen. In the season of our European triumph we were going well in the League as well as the Scottish Cup and Europe until United came to Pittodrie in mid-March and beat us 2-1. This was only three days after we had completed our 3-2 aggregate win over Bayern Munich in the Cup-Winners' Cup and I think the mental and physical effects of the workload we had to undertake at that period were a factor in losing to United. I've always thought that if that result had been reversed we could have won the League – United emerged champions by only a single point with only

A game Aberdeen would like to forget! Drew Jarvie is foiled by Dundee United keeper Hamish McAlpine during the 1979 Bells League Cup final replay in which United beat us 3-0.

goal difference separating Celtic and ourselves in second and third places.

On the other hand, if we had continued in the League running, it might have prejudiced our chances in both the Cup-Winners' Cup and the Scottish Cup, and, given the choice at the time, I would have gladly traded the Cup double we achieved for a League title.

Now that I think of it, I suppose Morton have more right to be regarded as Aberdeen's bogey team than Dundee United, considering that the Dons losing to the Greenock side would be considered more of an upset than defeat at United's hands. The concept of a particular ground rather than an opposing team being a bogey seems more acceptable to me, and I think it was visiting Cappielow that caused us most concern in meeting Morton. It is a depressing ground for the visiting team at the best of times and it seemed almost inevitable that as soon as our coach turned off the main road into the side street on which Cappielow is situated it would start raining, no matter how fine the weather had been up to that point.

Among the reverses which we have suffered there were those which brought an end to two of the record-breaking undefeated runs which I mentioned in the last chapter. Personally, though, my experience of Cappielow has been mixed. It was there that I made my first-team competitive debut with a substitute appearance in April 1973 and also my 500th first-team appearance almost exactly nine years later. On the first occasion Aberdeen won 2-1, but we lost by a similar margin in the 1982 game.

When we won the League Cup under Ally MacLeod it was, for most members of the side, the first taste of real success. Even getting to the final was regarded as a major achievement, but it was an achievement we had completed with a fair degree of style by going to Hampden in the semi-final and beating Rangers by a comprehensive 5-1 margin – with Jocky Scott claiming a hat-trick and Drew Jarvie, another member of our present management team, also contributing a goal with a shot from outside the box. That semi-final victory was so dear to us that we delayed our return to Aberdeen to relive it all over

Champagne in the bath as we celbrate clinching the Premier Divison title at Easter Road in May, 1980. That's me on the extreme right. I almost missed being in the picture.

again, going to the TV studios in Glasgow after the game to see it replayed.

Although our confidence for the final against Celtic was greatly boosted by beating Rangers so emphatically, we were under pressure from the Parkhead side for much of the final and we had to thank Drew for another goal which took the game into extra-time and Dave Robb, who replaced him, for scoring the winner in the second minute of the time extension.

Davie had been left out of the team for about half-a-dozen games before the final and I remember, on the bus on the way home, he kept aloof from the rest of the players, apparently still upset over his demotion. His winning goal, however, had proved his point and we could sense he was bursting with self-satisfaction, as well he might in the circumstances.

Our post-match celebrations that night were in the Station Hotel, Perth, where we broke our journey north for an overnight stay. There we dined royally on prawn cocktail and steaks, which I learned later was the winners' menu. Apparently the hotel had also prepared an alternative losers' menu – it was probably bread and water. Thankfully it wasn't required. I happen to be fond of prawn cocktail, so I was doubly glad that we had won at Hampden.

After that final, the celebration champagne made three vain trips to Hampden and returned unopened as we lost the Scottish Cup final in 1978 and then two successive League Cup finals, but when we clinched our first Premier Division title at Easter Road on 3 May 1980, we had travelled to Edinburgh unprepared for the celebrations which followed the game.

The omission was hardly surprising, for the pre-match situation was that we were a point behind Celtic with two games to go to Celtic's one. We were already far superior to the Celts on goal difference and that gap was enhanced by our 5-0 victory over Hibs, but the realisation that we had won the title dawned only when we heard that Celtic's final fixture,

Another triumphant procession through Aberdeen as Gordon Strachan, Peter Weir, Doug Rougvie and I display the Scottish Cup following our 1984 success.

against St Mirren at Love Street, had finished in a goalless draw. That made us champions, even if only on goal difference at that stage, a qualification which we subsequently removed in a 1-1 draw with Partick Thistle at Firhill four days later.

There was a dreamlike quality about that Easter Road game and for most of the players I think it took some time for the significance of the occasion to sink in. We could scarcely believe that it had really happened.

For some, it was even more special than for the rest of us: someone like Bobby Clark, for instance, who had played for Aberdeen since 1965, dreaming all the while of such a day. Clarkie's big regret on that occasion was that his father, a Clyde FC director and one of the 'keeper's most faithful fans, had not lived to share in the joy, having died a short time before.

I suspect that Clarkie knew about our title win a little ahead of the rest of us, for news of the Paisley game was going round the ground and I'm sure someone behind the goal was keeping him abreast of developments at Love Street, though he wasn't passing anything on to us at that stage.

When the realisation was finally absorbed, it was an emotional occasion. I remember Fergie, in his familiar camel coat, dancing across the Easter Road pitch when the final whistle sounded, and the later celebrations are marked down in my memory as the first and only time I have seen Stuart Kennedy partake of an alcoholic beverage.

We were, of course, to experience a League title triumph twice more in the next few seasons, setting new points records in each case, but whether it was familiarity or some other reason, I don't think either of these occasions quite matched up to the first for exhilaration.

Cup finals, too, tend to produce mixed feelings – and I don't just mean the difference between winning and losing them. They are great to play in, but sometimes the game itself seems to flash by and you cannot remember very much about it. This contrasts with the period before the final which seems to drag as the tension mounts. Probably you don't sleep too well the night before and all you want to do is get out on the park and into action. Then it is all over before you know it, although in our case we often gave ourselves the additional opportunity of extra-time in which to appreciate the sense of occasion, to say nothing of testing our phsyical fitness.

In the last three seasons we have maintained the Cup final habit with a couple of Skol Cup final appearances without being able to cap them with wins. On each occasion we were declared slightly unlucky to lose to Rangers, but there were, I feel, other, even more influential, factors which came into play. One of these, obviously, was the resurgence of Rangers as, once more, a real power in Scottish football. Another, I think, was the departure of Alex Ferguson from Pittodrie. You cannot break an association such as we had built up over a number of years with Fergie, who was really a master in those kind of situations, without something having to suffer. Possibly a combination of that and the Ibrox revival told against us.

CHAPTER NINE

Trial by TV

THE IDEA that "the referee has the last word" used to be one of the few football principles which met with universal acceptance, albeit with some reluctance by foolhardy players like myself who sometimes risk a yellow card in the fruitless pursuit of trying to get a match official to change his mind.

Recently, however, the Scottish Football Association, the game's ruling body in Scotland, raised a question mark over this fundamental principle in a move which could be interpreted as undermining the authority of referees.

I'm referring to the decision, taken by the SFA's Disciplinary and Referee Committee in January 1989, and ratified two months later by the full SFA Council, to ban two top-class referees, Kenny Hope and Louis Thow, from handling Scottish Cup ties for the rest of the season for what were considered lapses in their conduct of two different Premier Division games between Aberdeen and Rangers.

Leaving aside for the moment the particular circumstances of those two games, which were widely publicised at the time and which I'll be discussing in greater detail in the next chapter, the matter raises one or two wider issues. These include the referee supervisory system employed in Scotland and the extent to which television coverage of football matches contributes evidence, albeit unofficially, of misconduct on the field.

I don't know who decided initially that these referees had not done their job properly, but, according to newspaper reports at the time, the two cases were reported to the committee by the supervisors, who recommended a six-week total ban on the two referees. A few days later, the Scottish League Management Committee indicated a measure of disagreement with the Referee Committee's verdict by continuing to include Messrs Thow and Hope in the referees' ballot for League fixtures.

The referee supervisors are, for the most part, faceless people, and while they are presumably all former referees, one wonders how many of them have had experience of handling matches at this level. Judging a referee's performance against the theory of the textbook is one thing, but the gulf between theory and practice is as wide in refereeing as it is in anything else.

Was it fair, I wonder, to take action against these referees for alleged leniency without at the same time reviewing the "lenient" punishments imposed on the players concerned? Although I was the player principally involved in one of the cases, I would say that the referees did not deserve their cup-tie ban.

The "trial by TV" issue is certainly a thorny problem, and the ever-increasing number of matches which are being exposed to the camera's eye, with its associated mirror of play-back facilities, will only aggravate it. While the Referee Committee are limited to consideration of the referee's report in reaching their decision, the committee members would be less than human if they were not influenced, even subconsciously, by what they have seen on the screen.

One of the anomalies of television evidence is its unfair distribution. Those who play for one of the top teams are liable to a greater degree of exposure than their colleagues with the smaller clubs.

Television evidence may well one day be an accepted feature of football's disciplinary procedure and possibly also in the civil courts, but if that comes about, it is to be hoped that such evidence will be available for a player's defence as well as for his prosecution.

In this context, the person who suffers most from television coverage is, of course, the referee. His decisions have to be instant as he does not have the luxury of a replay of the incident which is afforded to the TV viewer.

Coming from me, this defence of the refereeing fraternity may surprise readers, but I'll have more to say on the subject of referees in the next chapter.

CHAPTER TEN

A Myth Exploded

IT SHOULD be said right away: I have no ambitions to be a football referee. In fact, I wouldn't have the referee's job for a Diego Maradona transfer fee.

I'm not sure exactly what gave rise to the myth that I want to referee every match I play in, but a myth it certainly is. The trouble is that anything repeated often enough eventually comes to be accepted as fact. As a joke it has gone a bit stale.

I'm not claiming to be completely innocent of the charge. I don't like losing and sure, I moan at referees when I don't agree with a decision, just as I moan at my team-mates when they make a mistake, but almost every team has at least one player who prefers to lead rather than be led, and I regard it as part of my function as Aberdeen's captain to represent my team's collective viewpoint. In doing so, I may on occasion get carried away and go a little too far in a heat-of-the-moment reaction, but it would be naive of anyone to imagine that I could hope to influence the referee. I KNOW that an experienced referee is hardly likely to pay attention to anything I have to say, but at the same time it's a good thing to remind him from time to time that you are there. It keeps him on his toes.

What the football public does not generally realise is that

Most eyeball-to-eyeball confrontations I have with referees are not marked with the smiles worn on this occasion by referee Bob Valentine and myself. It shows, however, that we're not always at daggers drawn.

some referees appreciate a bit of backchat between the players and themselves during a game, and sometimes even initiate it. This is particularly true of West of Scotland referees and is, I believe, a reflection of the Glasgow personality in which keeping up your end in a verbal contest is an admired quality.

The Hope brothers, Kenny and Dougie, are very much in this mould. They are both good referees and usually I get on well with them, although it may surprise the reader to learn that there are any referees who come into this category. In fact, there are quite a number with whom I'm on good terms. This is not really so astonishing, as over the years you get to know the top-class referees quite well.

Kenny Hope and his brother are what I would describe as Glasgow-type referees in that they don't mind you talking to them during a game. I think they try to mould their refereeing on the old style of official who could handle a situation without resorting to the yellow or red card, but by simply using their wit and personality.

My clash with Kenny in the Rangers-Aberdeen Premier Division game at Ibrox in November 1988 eventually brought him an SFA censure in the form of a Scottish Cup tie ban, but I think the whole incident was blown out of proportion by being highlighted on television. The bit that was screened gave the impression that I was doing all the talking, but I can assure you it was very much a two-way discussion.

I had been booked for a tackle on Kevin Drinkell. It was just about my first tackle of the game and I did not think it merited a yellow card. I was expressing the view that the referee had allowed himself to be influenced by the reaction of the Rangers' fans, for whom it is standard practice to bay for blood as soon as an opposing player makes contact with one of their own. Here was a case, I felt, where the crowd was guilty of the offence of which I am constantly being accused: trying to influence the referee – only they were having more success than I ever had!

Perhaps in the heat of the moment I was arguing my case more forcibly than I should have, but at no time in the conversation, heated as it may have been, did Kenny give me any indication that I was in danger of being sent off for expressing my views so frankly, and I wouldn't have expected such a threat from this particular referee.

Those who argued that I was lucky not to have been punished more severely were given extra ammunition when it seemed that Kenny and I were resuming our earlier argument as we left the field after the final whistle, although this was not featured by the television as the earlier incident had been.

In a sense, we were debating the same subject as before – the question of a refereeing decision being influenced by an external factor – but this time the argument was prompted by a separate incident. While lecturing Davie Dodds after giving a foul against him, the referee made it clear that Davie's offence was using his elbows. This angered me because I felt that the referee was being influenced by the disparaging remarks made about Davie's style of play by Rangers' manager Graeme

Souness after the Pittodrie clash of the two teams earlier in the season. Those remarks were made, I believe, with this specific aim in view and Kenny Hope was falling for the ruse. Kenny's only response to my complaint was: "don't be daft. Go away to your dressing-room." By that time Terry Butcher, the Rangers' skipper and a good friend of mine off the field, had intervened and persuaded me to give up the unequal contest. When I had cooled down, I realised that my approach to the referee had been too public and that a quiet word at another time might have been more effective. As far as I was concerned the matter was closed, but I wasn't surprised that the incident was featured in the Monday morning newspapers. The unprecedented action later taken against Kenny seems to discredit the unwritten rule that the referee should have the final word.

As I was not directly involved, I cannot comment too much

One of the flashpoints thrown up in a 1986 League game between Aberdeen and Rangers at Pittodrie. Former Don Doug Bell is the Rangers player receiving his marching orders from the referee. To complete an unusual coincidence, an Aberdeen player also sent off was a former Ranger Jim Bett.

on the controversy surrounding our Pittodrie meeting with Rangers six weeks before the Ibrox game. Team-mate Neil Simpson was the player at the centre of that furore following his tackle which led to the serious injury of Ian Durrant. It was a bad tackle, one which I'm sure will haunt Neil for a long time, but, again, the question of whether it merited a sending-off rather than the booking he received was purely a matter for the referee, Louis Thow, to decide on the basis of the incident as he saw it. The distinction to be drawn between a yellow and a red card as an appropriate punishment can be very fine indeed, and there arise in nearly every match instances where opinion would be evenly divided over the severity of a particular offence.

Regrettable as Simpson's challenge was, it scarcely justified the manner in which it was used by sections of the media to stir up a hate campaign against the player. The effect that this campaign had on Simmie's subsequent form is difficult to assess, but he was unsettled for the remainder of the season and eventually asked for a transfer to make a fresh start with a new club. Happily, the close season rest healed physical and mental injuries and he withdrew his request just before the start of the new season. Still, it must have been a harrowing time for him and his family.

It is probably more than a mere coincidence that the two incidents I have been discussing so far in this chapter both occurred in Aberdeen-Rangers clashes – as these fixtures seem to have gone hand in hand with controversy in recent years. The abnormally high incidence of sending-offs and bookings in Aberdeen-Rangers games – in 54 games between 1978 and the end of last season, 15 players (ten Rangers and five Aberdeen) have been ordered off, while the booking tally is 156 (87 Rangers, 69 Aberdeen) – which has encouraged many observers in the belief that there is a long-standing feud between the two teams. It has also been suggested that this ill-feeling dates back to the controversy surrounding the 1978-79 League Cup final and the clash between Doug Rougvie and Derek Johnstone which resulted in the Aberdeen player being sent off.

The latter theory, I think, can be discounted out of hand as ten years is a bit long for anyone to bear a grudge, particularly as there are very few survivors of that game left in either camp. As for the existence of a feud between Rangers and ourselves, I can only say that, as far as the Pittodrie players are concerned, we have never been aware of any particular antipathy towards our Ibrox rivals.

It is not easy, I admit, to account for the staggering crime count in these games in the past decade, but the reasons, I feel, are certainly less sinister than an ongoing vendetta.

In the first place, both clubs are usually challenging for domestic honours and meetings between them are consequently tense affairs with a lot at stake for either side. The high rate of success which we achieved against Rangers, particularly in League games, during the early and mid-'80s may have lent some desperation to the Ibrox players' efforts to change that pattern, which would account for considerably more Rangers than Aberdeen players featuring in the crime count. In the last two or three seasons, however, honours have been more evenly divided between the two sides and this swing has not been reflected in any noticeable increase in the number of Aberdeen players being sent off or booked.

Another possible factor could be that, with Rangers having had in recent years comparatively fewer players in the Scotland squad than formerly, Aberdeen's international players have had less opportunity of getting to know the Ibrox boys off the field. Gatherings of the international squad are good for promoting off-field friendships among players from different clubs and this is why, while Aberdeen-Celtic games are invariably tooth-and-nail encounters, there is rarely any lasting bad feeling.

In general, however, I think the bad behaviour record of Aberdeen-Rangers games can be attributed to a variety of causes, differing from game to game and each a one-off affair arising from particular circumstances in the game itself. The most unfortunate aspect of this bad record, of course, is that it figures prominently in pre-match publicity, and when a player is sent off or bookings are numerous, those incidents receive equally wide media coverage after the event.

I have a theory that my reputation as a surrogate referee started quite innocently in the readers' letters column of a national newspaper when a Rangers or Celtic supporter, seeking an excuse for his team's failure against Aberdeen, sent in a tongue-in-cheek letter suggesting that the Dons' success was due to Miller influencing the referee. This prompted other Old Firm followers to write in similar biased vein and it all snowballed from there.

What might have begun as a joke, however, has escalated out of all reasonable proportion and I am now saddled with an undeserved reputation as a would-be referee and a butt for after-dinner speakers. Having reached such a stage, I don't suppose there is anything I can say to persuade people otherwise. Mind you, I don't think the referees themselves believe the fiction that I put them under undue pressure, otherwise I would be booked more often. For a central defender, my disciplinary record is not too bad.

Perhaps it's a price I have to pay for my high profile in Scottish football. I'm rather a boring type in most respects and my willingness to chat with referee is maybe the only chink the critics can find in my armour. Whatever the answer, I'm convinced that my reputation, unwarranted and unwanted, was a major feature in provoking the extraordinary verbal attack which Dundee United manager Jim McLean launched on me in our Scottish Cup replay at Dens Park a couple of seasons ago. The Tannadice manager's action was, I'm sure, based on an unfortunate misconception of my actions.

Four minutes before the interval, Edinburgh referee Bill Crombie gave Paul Hegarty his marching orders for a two-footed tackle on Charlie Nicholas, and when the half-time whistle went, Jim McLean left his seat in the stand and made a bee-line for me as I left the field.

He obviously held me responsible for Paul's dismissal, accusing me of "running 70 yards" to badger the referee into sending the United player off. I rarely run as far as 70 yards in any circumstances, and what actually happened was that I ran 20 or 30 yards to see how badly Charlie had been hurt in the clash near the corner flag. As I passed the referee, I glanced towards him and could see he was intent on taking some action for he was actually moving away from the scene of the incident and beckoning Paul to follow him. To my mind, the referee had decided what he was going to do before I had even made a move.

When we came off the field at the interval, I did not notice the United manager until I was suddenly confronted by him, despite efforts by Alex McLeish to fend him off. It happened so suddenly that I was temporarily speechless (a rare event, I admit), but I remained perfectly calm – either through utter bewilderment over the manager's behaviour or my own absolute certainty that I had done nothing wrong, I don't know which – and this was indeed fortunate. The incident took place centre stage and if I had reacted as I might have done, as angrily as the aggressor, there could

The aftermath of the incident involving Dundee United manager Jim McLean and myself during a Scottish Cup replay at Dens Park. Manager McLean is shepherded away by Alex McLeish and Maurice Malpas while Aberdeen assistant manager Jimmy Mullen tries to calm me.

have been all sorts of nasty repercussions in crowd trouble.

My first thought was to put an end to Jim McLean's ranting and raving without the incident degenerating into physical violence. I turned away, looking for the referee as a possible peacemaker, but having attracted the official's attention, I turned back to see Jim McLean heading down the tunnel to the dressing-rooms.

The United manager, greatly as his achievements with the Tannadice club are to be admired, seems to have an unfortunate habit of letting his undoubted passion for the game get out of control and the severity of the punishment subsequently imposed on him for his outburst – a £4,000 fine and a three-year dugout ban – reflected his poor past record in this respect.

Before or since, I have never seen a manager attack a player of the opposing side in such a manner, and the only thing I can think of in mitigation is that Wee Jim must have been under tremendous pressure.

He scarcely improved his situation when, at the end of the game, he interrupted the Mr Superfit award presentation ceremony to make what could euphemistically be described as uncomplimentary remarks about the award-winner, Charlie Nicholas. That incident did not receive as much publicity as the earlier one, but it was undoubtedly taken into consideration by the SFA.

Later, some of my Pittodrie clubmates jokingly suggested that I should offer to pay a part of Jim McLean's fine, to which I replied that I would willingly serve some of his dugout ban. As a player, the dugout was one place I didn't want to spend time in.

There have been other refereeing controversies during my career in which my involvement has been less direct. Probably the most notable of these was the occasion referred to earlier when team-mate Doug Rougvie was sent off following a clash with Derek Johnstone during the 1978-79 League Cup final against Rangers.

I didn't see anything untoward in big Doug's challenge and I wasn't very far away at the time, but the one thing I am sure of is that referee Ian Foote certainly was not in a position where he could see any more than I saw, so his decision to put Doug off remains something of a mystery to me.

While on the subject of referees, I think the authorities could improve on-field relations between referees and players by establishing better lines of communication between the two bodies.

From time to time, the SFA launches a campaign aimed at reducing the incidence of a particular breach of the rules – tackling from behind, dissent, time-wasting are among the offences which have received special attention – and they instruct referees to be particularly strict in dealing with these cases. The only indication that we, the players, get that referees will be paying special attention to, say, tackling from behind, however, is a brief warning notice sent out by the SFA to the clubs and pinned on notice boards at the start of the season.

Wouldn't it be more effective for top referees, or the supervisors for that matter, to conduct seminars in different parts of the country to explain to the players the reasons for a particular purge and to discuss general topics of mutual concern? Such meetings would, I'm sure, get the message across much better than a couple of paragraphs on the notice board. Players meeting referees on an informal basis like this might also promote a better understanding between them and, if the supervisors were involved, they would no longer be derided as faceless people.

CHAPTER ELEVEN

European Ecstasy – and Agony

ABERDEEN fans are often criticised for appearing to be lukewarm in their vocal support of the Pittodrie side. This is another case of a reputation, whether deserved or otherwise, gaining credence through frequent repetition, a point I made on a more personal basis in the last chapter. The tradition can be fostered as a joke, as with the notion that all Aberdonians are mean, while in other instances the motives can be more malicious.

Speaking personally, there have been occasions when I have been disappointed by the level of support for the home team coming from a Pittodrie crowd, but, on the other hand, that same crowd contributed significantly to what was probably the most exciting evening I have experienced at the Aberdeen ground in my 18 years with the Dons.

European games at Pittodrie almost invariably produce a special atmosphere, but this one was extra special. The occasion, if you haven't already guessed, was the second leg of our European Cup-Winners' Cup quarter-final against triple European Cup-winners Bayern Munich in March 1983. Our appearance in the quarter-final stage of a European tournament for the first time in 12 campaigns made that tie a

Above, John Hewitt is acclaimed by Gordon Strachan after scoring the winning goal against Bayern Munich, while below, the Aberdeen players salute the Pittodrie fans for their contribution to a memorable evening.

milestone in the club's history and we gave ourselves every chance of progressing even farther with a 0-0 draw in the first leg in Munich's magnificent Olympic Stadium – arguably our finest away performance in Europe.

I have personal reasons for remembering the Munich game for it cost me a tooth. Executing one of his acrobatic hitch-kicks, Karl-Heinz Rummenigge connected with my face and knocked one of my front teeth clean out of my mouth. At least he had the courtesy to help me search for it on the pitch, even if, as we did so, he added insult to injury by asking if it was my own tooth or a false one. Our brief search failed and I have had to have several replacements since to fill the gap as artificial crowns are more easily displaced by knocks than the original was.

The atmosphere at a Pittodrie filled to capacity for the second leg was unbelievable. I have never encountered the like in my life and would have some doubts whether it will be matched. The fluctuations of the game itself – we twice came from behind – only heightened the drama. The Germans were leading 2-1 with 14 minutes to go when we struck back with an equaliser by Alex McLeish and took the lead through John Hewitt, who had been substituted for Neil Simpson, our first-half scorer. These two goals came within a minute of each other.

In the remaining 13 minutes during which we held on to that narrow lead, none of the Aberdeen players could fail to be inspired by the emotional vibrations coming from the crowd. The whole place was positively throbbing with excitement and the players expressed their appreciation to the supporters by returning to the pitch after the game had ended.

Accounting for a team of Bayern's calibre – and judging by what I saw on television of their recent meetings with Hearts and Rangers, they are still formidable opposition, though I think they had an even better team when we beat them – probably did more than anything else to convince us that we could go all the way in Europe that season.

And so it proved for we then went on to a semi-final victory over Waterschei, marred slightly by our only game lost in that

campaign, a 1-0 second-leg defeat in Belgium. This was possibly due to a combination of complacency after a runaway 5-1
win at Pittodrie and the consequent distraction of wondering
who our final opponents would be as Real Madrid and Austria
Vienna were meeting in the second leg of the other semi-final
the following evening.

If we as a team were disappointed by that defeat, irrelevant
though it was, the Genk game proved a tragedy for one of our
number. Stuart Kennedy took a knee injury which kept him
out of the final against Real Madrid, causing him to miss what
would have been a fitting climax to a distinguished football
career, and which eventually contributed to a premature end to
that career. Stuart was an outstanding full-back and if anyone
deserved to be in that European final, he did.

If the second leg of the Bayern tie tops my list for excitement, the Gothenburg final must rank as the most important
game I have played in, but that assessment comes only when it
is viewed in retrospect. At the time, I don't think any of us saw
it in its proper context as an occasion to be relished. There was
a little too much tension for that and the sense of achievement
in reaching the final of a European tournament for the first
time was enough to be going on with, while the fact that it
was a team of Real Madrid's unique reputation that we were
meeting was a bonus. Our confidence for that daunting task
couldn't have been higher.

One of the things that surprised me most about our preparations for Gothenburg was the attitude of our manager, Alex
Ferguson. Normally before big games, Fergie was like a cat on
hot bricks and the nervous cough – a sure sign of inward stress
– would make its appearance, but on this occasion the manager
was going about as if it were a friendly we were entering into.
It was so unlike his customary approach that I have since come
to the conclusion that his carefree attitude was a deliberate act
put on for our benefit. If that is the case, it was a performance
worthy of an Oscar and it certainly helped keep the players on
an even keel.

Beneath the surface calm, however, the manager was sparing
nothing to ensure that the preparations were as near ideal as

possible. A few days before departure for Sweden, for example, Fergie held a talk-in for the players' wives, who on this occasion were also travelling to the game instead of waiting anxiously at home. He explained to them that he did not want the players upset by any domestic worries and that, once the party was in Gothenburg, any messages they might have for their husbands should be passed through him. This applied even to Doug Bell's wife, who was expecting a baby round about the date of the final! Fortunately the newcomer's arrival was not ahead of schedule and there was no need to disturb Doug's pre-match concentration.

The presence of Jock Stein in our travelling party was a psychological plus. The Big Man had been through it all before in leading Celtic to their European Cup triumph in Lisbon and we knew that he would keep Fergie well advised of the possible pitfalls to avoid.

Every effort was made to create the perfect build-up to the final. Our headquarters, in the village of Farshatt outside the city, were admirably peaceful with walks along the river bank to contemplate the ducks for those so inclined. No pressure was put on us, apart from any that came from within ourselves, and a lively programme of quizzes and other light-hearted competitions ensured that there was no time for pre-match brooding. Our hotel was a magnet for various acquaintances we had not come across for some time. Thus we prepared in a relaxed atmosphere for what could be the greatest occasion of our sporting lives.

The events of the game itself do not require retelling in great detail, having been exhaustively chronicled elsewhere. To be perfectly honest, I found the Gothenburg match, like other finals I have played in, tended to be eagerly-awaited but then all over before it was fully appreciated – despite the fact that the historic victory over Real Madrid required extra time, a method of winning which was becoming almost habitual for us.

Torrential rain on the day of the final produced a threat, fortunately short-lived, of the game being postponed but, despite the Wimbledon-type covering system enjoyed by the

The extra-time goal by supersub John Hewitt which assured Aberdeen of the European Cup-Winners' Cup in Gothenburg . . . With the ball resting in the back of the net, John shows his delight in an aerial jig.
The trophy is ours and our joy is there for all to see . . . while back home in Aberdeen, this scene of celebration in the city centre was only one of many.

Ullevi Stadium pitch, the going was very heavy. These were conditions which probably suited us more than the Spaniards, but there was water lying about and this contributed to Real getting back on level terms after Eric Black had given us an opening goal. Taking advantage of a pass-back by Alex McLeish sticking on the soggy surface, Carlos Santillana looked certain to score until he was brought down by Jim Leighton..Juanita scored from the penalty spot.

I felt, however, that the longer the game went on, the stronger we became and our ability to handle that extra-time situation was proved when John Hewitt, who had been substituted for Eric Black, repeated his Bayern feat and claimed the winning goal in the 21st minute of the extension period.

With so much at stake, it was a tense game throughout and I was particularly aware of this playing at the back, where, remembering the earlier mistakes produced by the pitch conditions, we were conscious of the need to avoid any repetition. The final whistle eventually came as a blessed relief and all our tensions were released.

Our feelings throughout the aftermath to the final – the presentation of the trophy, the celebrations which followed, the trip home the following day, and the emotional reception we received back in Aberdeen – are difficult to describe, particularly now, more than six years later, but I think my chief emotion was a great sense of satisfaction. That may seem rather prosaic, but so much was happening all at once that it was only much later that we could fully appreciate our achievement.

If someone had asked me before the final what I would be doing if we won the European Cup-Winners' Cup, I would probably have said that I would be up all night celebrating but, in the event, it didn't quite turn out that way. When the team joined up with the wives at our hotel, I discovered that my wife Claire had had to retire to bed with a severe headache brought on by the excitement of the occasion. Fortunately, however, she recovered after about an hour's rest and we were able to join in the celebrations, but we didn't prolong them as most of us were feeling drained, mentally and physically, after an eventful day.

Aberdeen's Gothenburg triumph was historic, but it didn't just happen. For that particular Dons' team, it was the culmination of a European education spread over a number of seasons, during which every game against a foreign team – win, draw or defeat – contributed something to the learning process.

At the other end of the scale from the victory over Real Madrid there was the defeat we suffered against Liverpool almost three years earlier. Making our first appearance in the premier European tournament, the Champions' Cup, we did well to account for Austria Memphis in the first round, following a 1-0 Pittodrie win with a goalless draw in Vienna, but any illusions of grandeur we may have taken from beating the Austrians were rudely shattered when we came up against the English champions and were beaten in both legs.

The 1-0 defeat we suffered in the first leg was the first time in 16 European ties that Aberdeen had failed to score at Pittodrie and made Liverpool only the third team to win a European game at the Aberdeen ground. Worse than that, it produced a knee injury which deprived us of John McMaster for the remainder of that season. I'm convinced that, in the long run, John's top-class career was eventually curtailed by the injury he sustained in that clash with Ray Kennedy, to say nothing of it blighting his bright international prospects.

We had nothing to lose in the return leg at Anfield and the manager took the opportunity to give Neale Cooper, 19 days short of his 17th birthday, his European debut when he appeared as a late substitute for Doug Rougvie. Again, however, Liverpool were just too good for us and won 4-0, the first of their goals being supplied courtesy of a certain William Miller in the 37th minute. At that time the newspapers were having a field day in Miller own-goals as I was also blamed for putting the ball into my own net in games against St Mirren and Kilmarnock, but the Anfield goal was the only one I would regard as a genuine "o.g."! In trying a clearance following a corner, I mis-kicked and the ball came off the outside of my foot and into the net.

The Anfield game, however, produced one of those classic quotes, delivered in crisis, which stick in the memory. We went in at the interval three goals down on aggregate, but Drew Jarvie was one not easily disheartened. "Come on lads," he rallied us during the break. "Three quick goals and we're right back in this tie." It was a remark which reflected Drew's tremendous enthusiasm for the game, and although I don't think it was appreciated by many of us at the time, it has given us quite a few laughs over the years since.

Over the two legs against Liverpool we were well beaten, although the 5-0 aggregate scoreline probably flattered the English side slightly. The crucial difference between the teams, I felt, was their vast experience of European football and our lack of it. At that time we were rather naive in our approach to a competition which has its own unique set of requirements. This, however, was a shortcoming we set about remedying in the following years and our triumph in Gothenburg owed something to the lessons we learned from the Liverpool and other subsequent defeats.

I came to regard our meetings with West German teams

as a kind of yardstick by which to measure our European progress. In our early days under Fergie we were eliminated by Fortuna Dusseldorf (1978-79), Eintracht Frankfurt (1979-80) and SV Hamburg (1981-82), so when we accounted for Bayern Munich in 1982-83 I felt we had raised our standards sufficiently to have a chance of winning the tournament, and so it proved. I always considered the German teams were the hardest to play against. They have superb discipline and a high level of technical ability.

As I have already suggested, experience is an indispensable quality for European football – I don't think any club could win a European tournament without having a fair number of experienced players in their ranks – but European competitions also require the ability to adapt your style to the particular demands of these tourneys. For Scottish teams in particular, the desired style can be totally different from that employed in domestic football. Our success in the mid-80s was founded on having players who could make that transition effectively.

Doug Bell, for instance, had his finest hours for Aberdeen in European games. Continental teams didn't know what had hit them when Dougie started running at them with the ball. They were unaccustomed to players who were able to combine ball skill and direct aggression to the extent that he did. Then there was John McMaster with his ability to pinpoint long-range passes to telling effect.

For away games, Fergie's favourite formula was to pressurise the opposition as much as possible in the early stages of the game – not quite to the same extent as Dundee United have done over the years, but along similar lines – as this was the kind of football Continental teams were not used to, particularly when it happened on their home patch. Our brief was to win the ball back as quickly as possible after losing it to prevent the opposition keeping possession as they liked to do. If we were under steady pressure in these away games, Gordon Strachan was invaluable in affording the defence a breathing-space. We could win the ball, give it to Gordon, and be able to relax for long enough to regroup at the back while Gordon kept the opposition busy trying to pin him down in their own half.

Since our 1983 Cup-Winners' Cup triumph, our European ventures have produced flashes of success, such as claiming the Super Cup and at the same time avenging an earlier UEFA Cup defeat against SV Hamburg, but sadly they have more often ended in disappointment.

Probably the most keenly felt of these disappointments came the season after Gothenburg when we opened up the prospect of appearing in a European cup final two years in succession by again reaching the semi-final of the Cup-Winners' Cup only to lose to Porto. Although we were outplayed in the first leg in Portugal, we escaped lightly with a 1-0 defeat and thought we had a good chance of getting a favourable result at Pittodrie. But we were beaten again by a similar margin.

On a personal level, however, our 1985-86 European Cup campaign provided me with a highlight when, meeting IFK Gothenburg in the quarter-final, I made my 50th European

A rare sight as yours truly scores against IFK Gothenburg.

appearance in the first leg at Pittodrie and celebrated the occasion by scoring my second goal in Europe – the first had been against FC Sion in Switzerland three seasons earlier – in the course of a 2-2 draw. Unfortunately, we could do no better than a goalless draw in Gothenburg and went out on the away goals rule.

CHAPTER TWELVE

International Recollections

THE only full international match played at Pittodrie in the last quarter-century provided me with an introduction to international football. I hasten to add, however, that I didn't play in that game. I wasn't even in the Scotland squad. In fact, I was only 16½ at the time, and had been a professional footballer for only a few months.

The game was Scotland's European championship qualifier against Belgium in November 1971 and I, as a member of the Pittodrie ground staff, was on the pitch in the capacity of a ball boy!

The Scotland team that night, however, featured three of my Aberdeen club-mates in goalkeeper Bobby Clark, sweeper Martin Buchan and midfield man Steve Murray, while a fourth Aberdeen player, Willie Young, a late addition to the squad, was on the subs' bench. Also in the side was Hibs defender Pat Stanton, who some seven years later was to join us as assistant manager.

A goal by John O'Hare gave Scotland victory in this, the second game of Tommy Docherty's 15-month reign as Scotland manager, but the Pittodrie match was probably more significant as the start of the record-breaking international career of Kenny Dalglish, who gained the first of his 102 full caps when he appeared as a 47th-minute substitute for Alex Cropley. Apart from recognising his obvious talent, there was no way of foreseeing that November night that Kenny would compile such a colossal tally of caps, and little did I dream, as I did my share of retrieving the ball, that after serving my apprenticeship with half-a-dozen youth, ten Under-23, and a couple of over-age Under-21 caps, I would have the distinction of being one of the players among his contemporaries to come closest to Kenny's century of full caps. Even less did I envisage the supreme honour of captaining Scotland which I have now done on a dozen occasions.

I suppose in theory skippering an international team should not be all that different from skippering a club side, and I have always tried to tackle the two jobs in much the same way. The first thing, I think, is to make sure you are playing well yourself so that you can lead by example. Then you should try to get the best out of the players round about you, either by encouragement or by moaning at them as appropriate. This is where it is more difficult at international than at club level, mainly because you are usually not as familiar with international team-mates as with club-mates and you have to be a little more diplomatic in your approach.

I have never really felt that the Scotland captaincy was mine on a permanent basis – each manager has his own ideas of the qualities he is looking for in his choice of a captain – but I have always been happy to fulfil the deputy role when required. It has helped me accept this that all the Scotland captains I have served under have been players worthy of respect.

The Scotland skipper I would regard as being most like myself in his style of captaincy, and with whom I could identify most closely, was Billy Bremner. On the field, he was always very much involved in the action, liked to dictate the play and was not afraid to make decisions.

My strangest experience as captain of an international team came at Under-23 level when we played Holland in Breda in the first leg of a European Under-23 championship quarter-final in February 1976. The kick-off was delayed while we waited on the pitch for our opponents to come out of their dressing-room, and when they did eventually appear about ten minutes late I thought some of them were wearing strange shirts. We discovered later that the Dutch players had been holding a meeting with their association officials in an effort to get a share of the shirt sponsorship deal, and when the attempt failed some of the players wore their shirts inside out to hide the sponsors' name as a protest.

I had a more personal reason to remember that game, for at one stage I thought it was going to be my last. Taking an opponent's elbow right on my Adam's apple, I thought at first I had swallowed my tongue as I struggled for breath. It was very painful to breathe for some time afterwards. Possibly my injury was part of the price to be paid for having Kenny Burns as a team-mate, for earlier in the game he had made his presence felt, kicking all and sundry on the opposing side. It had to be me who suffered the backlash.

With the Dutch Under-23s leading 2-0, we thought there might be a chance of a match abandonment saving us from our first defeat in eight games. The Dutch crowd showed their displeasure with the referee by raining bottles down on the pitch, but the referee pointed out that the missiles were only relatively harmless plastic bottles and not glass ones as we thought.

The second leg of that quarter-final was played at Easter Road five weeks later when our 2-0 win produced a 2-2 draw after extra time – but Holland won through to the semi-final 4-3 on penalties. John Brownlie, Frank Gray and I scored from the spot, but Joe Jordan and Tommy Craig had their efforts saved.

Mention of my Easter Road penalty conversion reminds me of other – less happy – occasions at club level when I have been involved in penalty-kick deciders, reluctantly, I may add, because I have never regarded myself as a spot-kick expert. When it comes down, however, to a result hanging on the outcome of a penalty shoot-out, it is seldom easy to get the necessary five volunteers for the nerve-testing duty, and I have felt that my responsibility as skipper outweighs any lack of confidence in my own ability to score from the spot.

The first of these sad occasions was the second leg of the European Cup first-round tie against Dynamo Berlin in East Berlin in October 1984. Failing to make the most of our scoring chances in the first leg at Pittodrie, we went behind the iron curtain with only a 2-1 lead and the East Germans won by a similar margin to make penalties necessary.

We were given an edge when Dynamo's third spot-kick struck the crossbar and our first four takers, Ian Porteous, Tommy McQueen, John Hewitt and Billy Stark all scored, although Billy had to go through the nerve-racking experience of retaking his kick after scoring at the first attempt. I had only to convert the fifth penalty and we were through, but Bodo Rudwaleit, Dynamo's giant goalkeeper, saved my shot, hit fairly hard to his right-hand side. While waiting for my turn, I had decided to side-foot the ball to the keeper's left, but, for some reason, changed my mind on the way from the centre circle to the penalty spot – and paid the price for indecision.

Level with four penalty goals each, we went into sudden death penalties and Dynamo went through when Rudwaleit also saved Eric Black's effort and the Germans' sixth man scored. Although it was actually Eric's failure which put us out, my earlier miss seemed to attract most of the criticism surrounding our dismissal, which, I suppose, was fair enough as I could probably handle it better than Eric, who had celebrated his 21st birthday only two days earlier.

Not everyone, however, blamed me. When we arrived back at Aberdeen Airport, an elderly woman fan had a kind word of sympathy for me. "Never mind, Willie," she said, and I wished I could dismiss the memory as readily as she obviously could.

After the Berlin experience, I promised my wife Claire that if a similar situation arose again I would not be one of the penalty-takers. Such a promise was probably tempting Fate and, sure enough, I was faced with the dilemma again just under two years later when our Skol Cup quarter-final with Celtic at Pittodrie produced a 1-1 draw after extra time. Again we had the familiar problem of finding five players willing to take the penalties and I admit that, after my earlier experience, I was one of the most reluctant. In the end, I think it was that feeling of responsibility – plus a little prodding from Alex Ferguson – that saw me roped in.

Jim Leighton gave us an excellent start by saving Celtic's first penalty from Roy Aitken but John Hewitt and I both failed from the spot and with Maurice Johnston, Peter Grant, Owen Archdeacon and Brian McClair all netting, Celtic were through 4-2 without our fifth penalty-taker being required. Jim Bett and Peter Weir were our successful takers. This time I stuck to my decision to send the spot-kick to the goalkeeper's left, but Pat Bonner guessed correctly and managed to stop the shot – and I was in the doghouse at home for breaking my promise.

Another year passed and we were back in a losing penalty situation after a 3-3 extra-time draw with Rangers in the 1987-88 Skol Cup final. I was not directly involved on this occasion, but Peter Nicholas had my full sympathy when his attempt glanced off the crossbar. There was also a pang of guilt because if Peter had not agreed to be a penalty-taker, I could well have found myself in the firing line once more. Perhaps I should have been there!

To return to the Under-23 international at Easter Road after this digression, that penalty was my first international goal and the only other time I achieved the feat was in a full international at Hampden Park. The second goal proved more fruitful than the first as it gave Scotland a 1-0 victory over Wales in a home championship match in May 1980.

The following year's home championship meeting with Wales, at Swansea, was another memorable occasion, but not so much for the game itself as for the roundabout way Alex McLeish and I got to it.

Fog at Aberdeen Airport prevented us joining the rest of the Scotland squad in Glasgow and our take-off was switched to the Lossiemouth RAF station, so it was a case of coach from Aberdeen to Lossie, a flight from there to London, train from London to the squad's headquarters in Porthcawl and finally a taxi to the hotel.

As we were waiting to take off at Lossiemouth, the captain came round to reassure the passengers. "We've had a little trouble with one of the engines, but if you keep your fingers crossed, we hope to take off soon," he told us. The idea of a pilot depending on his passengers keeping their fingers crossed did not exactly fill me with confidence about our safety, but we made it to London without mishap. Altogether it hadn't been a very auspicious start to the trip for earlier, when I had phoned to let Jock Stein know of our problems, he didn't sound over-joyed by the news and the only sympathy I got from him was a growl of assent for our new travelling arrangements.

Our luck did not improve either – we suffered a 2-0 defeat. Alex was slightly less unfortunate for he was left on the bench and I remember consoling him with the suggestion that missing that game was probably the best thing that could have happened to him in view of the result. My words proved prophetic as he was back in the team for the following week's games against Northern Ireland at Hampden and England at Wembley, both of which we won.

As I mentioned earlier, captaincy frequently involves making decisions on the field, but I can recall an occasion when one of my decisions led to Richard Gough being replaced. It was in the friendly against France in Marseilles in June 1984.

Jock Stein was employing a five-at-the back defence, a system which, not for the first time, I had grave reservations about as being the most effective for this particular opposition. France had a very good team at that time and were playing with only one up front but with skilful midfield players all capable of coming through. I felt that these players should be picked up early, but our defensive set-up allowed them too much space to build attacks.

We were given a roasting in the first half and with no improvement after the interval, I suggested to Richard that he should move farther forward to pick up any of the French midfield players coming through. He readily agreed as he also appreciated our system wasn't working, but within ten minutes of the change, the manager took Richard off and substituted

Charlie Nicholas for him, effectively confirming the four-at-the-back system to which I had changed. Richard's change of role apparently singled him out as the candidate for replacement.

Before the kick-off of that game, I found myself shaking hands with the great Michel Platini as we met for the toss-up. He took me aback when he asked if I would like my photograph taken, gesturing to a photographer hovering nearby. Delivered in the air of bestowing a great favour, it was the kind of question normally asked of a team mascot rather than the opposing captain.

Then when the game ended with Scotland beaten 2-0 – and flattered by that scoreline – I saw Platini approaching me and thought for a few seconds that he was coming to exchange shirts. He passed me by, but my disappointment was short-lived for when I looked round he was handing his shirt over to Neil Simpson, who had been substituted for Gordon Strachan at the interval, and had consequently been the player in direct opposition to the French captain in the second half.

I don't approve of the practice in the closing stages of international games of players shadowing the prominent players in the opposing team to be on hand for the traditional exchange of shirts at the final whistle. If someone offers me an exchange, I'll always accept, but otherwise I like to swap with the player I'm playing against. As this was what Platini was doing, I had no complaints although I must admit that it was only Simmie getting the shirt which prevented me from being disappointed. As I said, the French had only one player up front that night, so I think I ended up changing shirts with one of their substitutes.

The World Cup finals in Spain in 1982 and Mexico four years later, of course, provided me with many memories, happy and otherwise.

The visit to Spain, for example, had a disappointing start for me when I was only on the bench for the opening game against New Zealand in Malaga, with Allan Evans and Alan Hansen as the central defensive pair. Although we finished 5-2 winners in that game, the reader may recall that the loss of two goals eventually proved an expensive luxury in our bid to qualify for the second phase,and after watching a re-run of the game on television, I was convinced that I could possibly have prevented both New Zealand goals had I been playing. That may sound big-headed but the build-up to the New Zealand goals was such that on each occasion I would normally have been lying deeper than either of the central defenders and thus in a position where I could have made a successful challenge.

As I've said, those two New Zealand goals were particularly expensive. They could have made all the difference between Scotland qualifying and not qualifying for the second phase. After a 4-1 defeat against Brazil in Seville in the second game, we needed to beat Russia in the last first-phase match to go through on points, but had to settle for a 2-2 draw. That was good enough for the Russians to progress on goal difference, along with Brazil, but if we had not conceded two goals to New Zealand, we would have equalled Russia's plus-two goal difference and would have had the advantage in having scored more goals (eight to Russia's six).

The incident which is always recalled from that game is, of course, the collision between Alan Hansen and myself which led to Shengalia scoring the goal which gave Russia a 2-1 lead. It was a simple misjudgment of the type which could occur in any game, but it gained everlasting notoriety from a combination of circumstances: its consequences in the loss of a goal and the degree to which it influenced the outcome of a game so vital to Scotland's qualifying chances.

After missing the New Zealand game, I was particularly determined to do well against the Russians, and, in fact, I still reckon it was one of my best international performances. I was even more involved in the play than usual for a sweeper, getting in good tackles and maintaining my concentration. Everything seemed to be going for me.

My memory of the clash with Alan Hansen is that he went to meet a high ball down the touchline. It seemed to me that the ball was going over his head, so I went to cover it, but, by running backwards, Alan just managed to get a touch to the ball – just enough to deflect it past me – before he himself

The Aberdeen contingent in the Scotland squad for the second leg of the World Cup qualifying match against Australia in Melbourne in December, 1985: Alex McLeish, Neale Cooper, Stewart McKimmie and I gather round Jim Leighton.

crashed into me and we both went down, allowing Shengalia freedom to run on and score.

How that game would have resulted if that incident had not occurred is a matter of pure speculation, but it was, of course, claimed that our crash had cost Scotland a place in the second phase. I still feel that the damage was done by conceding two goals against New Zealand in the opening match.

I was more fortunate in the 1986 finals, playing in all three first-phase games and captaining the side in the last of these, against Uruguay in the Neza Stadium.

I thought we were a bit unlucky in the opening game to lose to Denmark by the only goal, but what impressed me most in that match was the quality of the players we were up against. At the time I thought that Preben Elkjaer got a lucky rebound of the ball when he scored the decisive goal, but after watching him on television a few times since, I have come to the conclusion that he does it too often for it to be purely luck.

It's difficult to explain what I mean without becoming too technical, but briefly what happened on that occasion was that the Dane broke clear with the ball with only myself and the goalkeeper to beat and I had to balance delaying my challenge as long as possible to let the other defenders get back with getting in a tackle at the moment he was most vulnerable to it. When I decided the moment had come just outside the box, the ball seemed to bobble between us, rebound off his shin, but still fall in his path. He blasted it at an acute angle across the face of the goal where it hit the far post and went into the net.

Elkjaer can consistently retain possession in such circumstances and I think it's because he's a big fellow and he keeps his body well over the ball when running with it close to his feet. When he is tackled, the closeness of the ball to his feet, legs and lower body, together with his considerable forward momentum, increases the chance of the ball rebounding off some part of his body and falling right for him.

I can think of only one player in Scotland who could be likened to Elkjaer in his ability to profit from this apparently lucky break of the ball and that is former Aberdeen team-mate Mark McGhee, now back with Newcastle United.

The second game, against West Germany in Queretaro, was memorable for me, of course, because it marked my 50th full cap, but the abiding memory of that game was an amusing one. After scoring the goal which gave us an early lead, Gordon Strachan made as if to emulate the practice of some of the continental stars, who celebrate scoring by hurdling the advertising boards surrounding the playing area to take the crowd's acclaim. In Gordon's case, however, he decided that clearing the boards was too risky a venture for someone of his diminutive stature so he contented himself with swinging one leg on top of the barrier and resting it there while giving the crowd an expressive shrug to indicate that that was the best he could do.

Much less amusing were some of the comments which my former manager Ally McLeod was reported to be making in the newspapers at home while we were in Mexico. During one of my telephone calls home, Claire reported that Ally was quoted as saying that I should be left out of the team against West Germany and replaced by Dave Narey (who, as it turned out, came into the team for that game when Alex McLeish was ruled out by illness). Ally was, of course, perfectly entitled to his opinion, but it irritated me that someone who had had such bitter experience of being involved in World Cup finals halfway round the world and unable to defend himself against criticism at home should allow himself to be quoted in such a way about someone in a similar position. Ally, of all people, really should have known better.

On a later occasion – I think it was following Holland's success in the 1988 European championships – Ally again came out with what I considered an ill-judged comment on the Scotland team selection, this time directed against two of his former charges in Alex McLeish and myself. He wanted Scotland to adopt Holland's style of play and his theory was to field Liverpool pair Alan Hansen and Gary Gillespie in central defence instead of Big Alex and myself. That may be OK if, like Holland, you have world-class players throughout the side, but to suggest that Scotland's problems could all be solved simply by playing two skilful central defenders is naïve in the extreme and someone with Ally's managerial experience at both club and international levels should appreciate that.

To get back to the Mexico World Cup finals, the first-phase situation was, for us, almost a repeat of that in Spain four years earlier, Scotland going into the final Group E game

Home again . . . Teddy Scott and I at Aberdeen Airport after the 1986 World Cup finals in Mexico.

110

requiring a win over Uruguay to have a chance of qualifying.

Probably the worst thing that could have happened to us was Uruguay having a player sent off in the opening minute of the game. When the opposition is reduced to ten men, it frequently upsets the pattern of the full-strength team. It's as if they say to themselves: "We have an extra man here. What are we going to do with him?"

In these circumstances, it is necessary for someone to take control of the situation, and, with hindsight, it was perhaps a mistake for Alex Ferguson to leave Graeme Souness out of the side for that game. I'm sure that the manager's pre-match reasoning was that Graeme, one of the older members of the squad, had had two games in energy-sapping conditions and Fergie wasn't to know that the opposition would be reduced to ten men for most of the game. When they were, however, Graeme could have been just the person as the extra man and with his experience he could have taken full advantage of the situation instead of us having to endure a goalless draw.

It was a brave decision by Fergie to leave out one of his senior, and potentially most influential, players, but I'm absolutely convinced that, at the time, he believed it was the right thing to do. It has been suggested that there had been off-the-field conflict between Graeme and the manager and that this contributed to his omission, but I know Fergie too well to give any credence to the idea that he would allow any dispute, if indeed there was one between them, to influence his selection.

Close-season international tours provoke a mixed reaction among professional footballers. Some view them as something to be endured rather than enjoyed, maybe even a waste of time – time which after a long, hard domestic season could be more profitably and pleasurably spent relaxing at home or on a family holiday. It is remarkable how many players selected for such tours suddenly fall victim to unspecified end-of-season "injuries" which force their "reluctant" withdrawal from the tour party.

For others, however, these trips are attractive, offering, perhaps, visits to new countries where friendly games can be played without too much pressure, and providing opportunities to strengthen claims for a regular place in the Scotland team.

The latter attitude would be the one I'd identify with. I have often thought that I did my international prospects no harm on Scotland's east European tour in May 1980 when I played against both Poland and Hungary. Although we lost both games, my place in the national side seemed a little more secure after that tour.

The Polish part of the tour also turned out to be something of a political education. The Gdansk shipyard workers, led by Lech Walesa, were at the time just beginning to introduce the word "Solidarity" into the world's newspaper headlines and most of us arrived in Poznan knowing little or nothing about the miserably poor living conditions which existed there then. We assumed that, with Poland being an Eastern Bloc country, the Poles would be very close to their Russian neighbours in their outlook.

It was, of all things, a visit to a cinema which did most to dispel that impression. We were going to see a film entitled, according to our female interpreter, *The Stranger*, which turned out to be her understandable mistranslation of the well-known film *The Alien* but it was the accompanying newsreel which proved the most enlightening part of the programme.

One item in the newsreel captured the visit to Poland of a top-ranking Russian politician to inaugurate a new road system or something like that, but as soon as he appeared on the screen, the whole cinema erupted into a bedlam of catcalls and whistles. The audience really gave the Russian gentleman pelters. The abuse gradually changed to derisive laughter as the soundtrack of the Russian's speech was heard. We couldn't, of course, understand the finer niceties which the Poles obviously thought hilariously funny until the interpreter explained that the visiting dignitary had been extolling the generosity of Russia in giving Poland this new road system.

That, of course, was before the days of *glasnost* and *perestroika*, but I wonder how much the present situation has changed.

Very different from the 1980 tour was my second close-season overseas trip with Scotland. That was the visit to Canada in June 1983 when we played three games against the national side in different parts of the country, winning them all without conceding a single goal. I skippered Scotland in the opening game in Vancouver, but Graeme Souness, who made only a substitute appearance in that game, resumed the captaincy for the two other matches.

My own performance in Canada brought conflicting reactions. The Scottish Press selected me as "Player of the Tour" and presented me with a quaich, while I was criticised by the Canadian manager, a former England player, for "tackling too hard". You just can't win!

The Canadian boss was probably looking on the games as friendlies, but I certainly wasn't. To me it was a chance to further my international career. I still couldn't quite understand his complaint because one of the games was played on astroturf which ruled out what we would regard as hard tackling.

Socially, however, the Canadian trip was most enjoyable. Former Pittodrie team-mate Duncan Davidson, who had played in Canada, provided me with introductions to several of the Canadian internationals and with our playing them three times we got to know them quite well.

This random collection of incidents from my international career would not be complete without some reference to what I regard as one of the most significant of my caps. It was my 64th, and it came against Yugoslavia in Zagreb only a short time before the publication of this book.

Considering Scotland were beaten 3-1, it might not be considered a particularly auspicious occasion to recall, but, for me, it was very important as it marked the resumption of my place in the Scotland team after missing six internationals, including three World Cup qualifying ties, due to injury, and it came at a timely stage in our efforts to take Scotland to their fifth successive World Cup finals series.

In the context of the international team, things can change very quickly, but I felt that my comeback went well despite the match result and there was the added satisfaction of rejecting any suggestion that my knee operation had terminated my challenge for a place in the Scotland side.

It seems likely that any reservations Andy Roxburgh might have had about recalling me after an eight-month absence were banished by my club form in the opening weeks of the new season. The success of this parallel return for club and country owed much, I felt, to extra training I put in during the close season, realising how much depended on the start I made to the season.

CHAPTER THIRTEEN

They Shall Not Pass

IT MAY be that, like good marriages, good football partnerships are made in heaven, but they, just like a successful marriage, do not thrive without a lot of hard work being put into them. That, at least, has been my experience with particular regard to the happy defensive partnership I have enjoyed with Alex McLeish and Jim Leighton over a number of years at both club and international levels.

Before going any farther, however, I want to make it clear that any reputation which Aberdeen has attracted for having a sound defence is not due entirely to the threesome I have mentioned. The best of combinations at the heart of the defence could be harassed into mistakes if the opposition's wide players are consistently flying past your full-backs and firing in crosses. We have been lucky at Pittodrie in having first-rate support from a series of highly competent full-backs, players such as Stuart Kennedy, Doug Rougvie – big Doug may have had his critics among the purists, but he is a first-class defender – John McMaster, and more recently, Stewart McKimmie, David Robertson and Ian Robertson.

To return to my original point, however, the "Pittodrie Triangle", as it has been called, did not just happen of its

*Jim Leighton, Alex McLeish and myself ... an effective defensive
partnership at club and international level.*

own accord, although it may have seemed that way to the casual observer. All three of us had to work on the partnership's
development, learning from our mistakes – the obvious and the
not so obvious – and, probably most importantly, discussing
and analysing each game in detail afterwards.

The fact that Jim and Alex both became first-choice regulars
in the first team in the same season (1980-81) could have made
integration into the side more difficult, but, fortunately, both
had profited from fairly extensive spells of first-team duty at
some time in the preceding two seasons.

In each case, it was injury to established first-team players
which initially gave them their chance in the first season of
Alex Ferguson's managership – 1978-79. Jim deputised for
Bobby Clark when he fractured a thumb in a pre-season
friendly against Tottenham a few weeks before his testimonial
match and Alex took over the number five shirt when Willie
Garner broke a leg in the European Cup-Winners' Cup-tie
against Marek Dimitrov in Bulgaria in mid-September. When
Bobby and Willie recovered from their respective injuries later
that season, Jim and Alex resumed their reserve-team careers.

The limitations of being a goalkeeper meant that, apart from a few odd first-team appearances in 1979-80, Jim had to wait until the 1980-81 season before finally succeeding Bobby, who had in the intervening season fulfilled a long-cherished ambition by sharing in Aberdeen's League Championship triumph.

As an outfield player, however, Alex had other options open to him and Fergie, realising that this big, red-headed 20-year-old was too good a player to leave out of the first team simply because his natural position was already competently occupied, used him in a midfield role. Actually big Alex missed only nine of the Dons' 66 games in the 1979-80 season.

On the few occasions that Willie Garner was not available, Alex had Doug Rougvie as a rival for the number five shirt, but towards the end of that season he was beginning to wear it more regularly. It was at centre-half that Alex found himself right from the start of the 1980-81 season – and he's been there ever since, give or take the odd absence through injury or suspension. This was no reflection on the ability of Willie Garner, who did not languish in the reserves for long before being snapped up by Celtic where he rejoined his former boss and admirer Billy McNeill.

It was not only Aberdeen club managers Ally MacLeod, Billy McNeill and Alex Ferguson who were quick to recognise the great potential of Alex McLeish. After being given his international baptism by Ally in an Under-21 game against Wales in February 1978, he gained further Under-21 experience with Ally's successor as Scotland manager, Jock Stein, before winning his first full cap against Portugal in March 1980 while I tried to contain my impatience on the substitutes' bench.

As I've mentioned elsewhere, I felt that Alex was one of the Big Man's favourites and I used to wind him up by telling him he was playing for Scotland because he bore a strong resemblance to Jock's own son. I was, of course, joking, but there may have been a touch of sour grapes about the kidding because I certainly wasn't one of Jock's favourites – not at that time anyway.

By the time Alex came into the Aberdeen first team, I had had reasonably successful central defensive partnerships with, in succession, Willie Young, Eddie Thomson and Willie Garner, and in the initial stages of the McLeish-Miller combination, I was very much the senior partner, breaking in the new boy in big Alex. "Boy" is the operative word for although Alex was 21 by the time we came together on a regular basis, he didn't look even that age, as I was reminded recently when searching through old photographs for the purpose of this book. Looking at him now, it's difficult to believe how much his boyish good looks (I'm flattering him again) have been changed into craggy maturity by the addition of a few dozen facial scars, each one a tribute to a fearless header of the ball.

With the passage of time, Alex has gained experience and we have become used to each other's play. It has now become an equal partnership, with each knowing where the other will be and what he will be doing in any given set of circumstances – the type of instinctive knowledge which only long experience working together can bring.

Our partnership started off with several advantages, not least that Alex is a genuine centre-half while I'm essentially a sweeper. As such, I prefer to have my partner playing in front of me, attacking the ball, rather than playing alongside me in a twin centre-half situation. This has posed something of a problem for me to overcome throughout my international career. While at club level I have always played as sweeper – behind my central defensive partner – with no complaints from the manager, most Scotland managers I have played under have at some time or other wanted to operate with a squarer defensive system, with the central defenders playing alongside each other.

In this context, I was particularly interested in the remarks of Ted Croker at the Scottish Football Writers' Association dinner last May. Mr Croker, who had recently retired after a long spell as secretary of the English Football Association, was advocating that English football should "follow the example of successful continental countries such as Italy and Holland and adopt the sweeper system" as one of the answers to the game's ills in England. He obviously didn't appreciate that there was no need to cross the Channel to find an example of that particular defensive system in operation. It is fairly common practice here in Scotland. At the same time, it was satisfying to hear a prominent and experienced football official backing up my view that having a sweeper at the back is more effective than the flatter defence favoured on the other side of the border.

To return to Alex McLeish, his natural height advantage, allied to superb timing, means that Alex very rarely fails to win the ball in the air and, in fact, I would rate him the best header of the ball from the long clearance I have come across anywhere in the world. He is, perhaps, not quite as accomplished in going to win a high ball from, say, a driven corner or a driven shot forward, and, in his earlier days, he was slightly weak on the ground. That weakness, however, has been eliminated by hard work, and now he is good in the air, good on the ground and an able tactician with bags of experience behind him. Altogether, he is without doubt the best centre-half in Scotland and maybe even Britain, and one of the best central defenders in Europe.

Our partnership has certainly been helped by the fact that we get on with each other as well off the park as on it. Although we're almost totally different in personality, our individual characteristics are compatible and we complement each other. That does not mean that either of us misses a chance to take the rise out of the other. Alex at every available opportunity, public and otherwise, gets in a crack about the fatness of my wallet – he thinks that because I have business interests as well as being a professional footballer, I must be loaded. How wrong he can be only another businessman could tell. And I must say he hasn't been so ready with the wallet remarks recently since I've been giving him a taste of his own medicine by offering to help him count the proceeds of his testimonial year.

For many years now, Alex and I have roomed together when travelling with either Aberdeen or Scotland squads. On these occasions, I like to spend my free time in my room, reading a book, watching television or just sleeping, and Alex rarely interferes with any of these activities because he is very rarely in the room for long. A restless type, he is usually visiting some of the other rooms engaged in one of his frequent practical jokes, winding up some of the other players or hatching mischief of one kind or another.

I'm maybe giving away secrets now, but one of his favourite ploys whenever we stayed overnight in Glasgow and there was anyone in the party for the first time was to phone the newcomer's room, assume a false voice, and pretend to be a well-known Glasgow sports reporter seeking an interview.

If the victim accepted the call as genuine, sooner or later Alex would introduce a loaded question such as, "I'm told that Alex McLeish is not playing well at the moment. Do you think he is over the hill?" or, "They say that Willie Miller is beginning to show his years. How long do you think he'll last?" Overawed by being interviewed by a big-name journalist, the young player might be tempted into agreeing with his questioner, little suspecting that listening on the other end of the line were some of the older members of the team, including the person he was being invited to find fault with.

Some notable successes were achieved by this con trick, but one newcomer we failed completely with was Brian Irvine. The big defender staunchly refused to "knock" any of the players who might be regarded as standing in his way for a first-team place. We couldn't get Brian to say a bad word about anyone.

The difference in personality between Alex and myself is possibly best illustrated by our conversations with casual acquaintances. The prominent footballer is a natural target for anyone who has a theory on the game to propound or a grievance to air. I don't mind chatting about football to anyone, but once they have told me their views and heard mine, that's the conversation exhausted as far as I'm concerned. Alex, however, seems to collect these people and gets on famously with them, often exchanging telephone numbers before parting.

I must admit it took a little longer to create a good working relationship with Jim Leighton than it did with Alex McLeish and we did have a few misunderstandings in the early stages of his first-team career.

One of these produced the "own goal" in the game against St Mirren which I referred to in discussing the Liverpool European Cup-tie. On that occasion, Jim came off his goal-line and in his attempt to get at the ball, he collided with me. The ball came off my shin and went into the net.

Earlier that season, in another game against St Mirren, this time in the Drybrough Cup final at Hampden, Jim again rushed out of his goal as I was challenging an opponent on the edge of the box and between us we managed to concede a penalty which Frank McDougall converted. Fortunately this did not deprive us of victory, Steve Cowan snatching the winner, but it was a goal which could have been avoided and in conjunction with the "own goal" incident, it prompted us to devise definite rules to meet these situations.

The most important of these rules, in essence, dictated that Jim should remain on his line, or at least confine himself to his six-yard box at all times unless it was obvious that none of the other defenders had a hope of catching an opposing player once he had broken through. It was also understood that the keeper should never move outside the line of his goalposts to take a pass-back. This was to reduce the chance of the ball finding the goal-line unprotected in the event of the defender misdirecting his pass-back.

Once these early snags were sorted out, the understanding between Jim, Alex and myself developed apace and we went on to form an excellent partnership over a seven-year period before Jim's departure for Old Trafford. We were, however, always working on its improvement.

Going back to the beginning of that period, Jim had joined the Pittodrie rearguard with an important advantage: a wealth of goalkeeping knowledge passed on to him by Bobby Clark, his predecessor as Aberdeen's number one keeper. The extent to which Bobby shared with reserve keepers Jim Leighton and John Gardiner the fruits of his great experience never ceased to amaze me. Bobby, of course, was a born coach and loved passing on his knowledge and advice to others, but it also, I think, demonstrated his tremendous generosity of spirt. While I'm always willing to give any young player advice, I doubt whether in similar circumstances I would do as Bobby did and reveal *all* my secrets to someone who could use them to help displace me. It would be a lot to ask of any outfield player, but even more in the case of a goalkeeper for, after all, there is room for only one keeper in a team.

Having lost Jim Leighton to Manchester United, it was a major surprise to me – and to most other people at Pittodrie, I dare say – that we should find such an able successor as Theo Snelders, particularly as he came to Aberdeen as a relatively unknown quantity. The tremendous impact which the Dutchman has made on Scottish football, and particularly on the players who came up against him, was underlined when he was voted "Player of the Year" by the Scottish Professional Footballers' Association.

Playing, in a short period, in front of two keepers whom I would rate as world-class has, however, afforded me an interesting opportunity to draw comparisons. Jim was never particularly athletic or fast on his feet, although these were aspects he worked on to improve, but on his goal-line few keepers can rival him as a saver of shots from either close range or farther out. Theo has a much more impressive physique, and his command of cross balls is superior, particularly those to the back post. I never felt that Jim was completely comfortable with overhead balls swinging in towards the far post.

Before Theo's arrival, I was rather dreading the prospect of breaking in a new goalkeeper to our defensive set-up, but in the event the big Dutchman fitted in relatively easily. The "stay on your line except as a last resort" instruction did not give him any trouble because he did not seem to be a keeper who liked to rush off his line.

We at Pittodrie could scarcely credit our good fortune in getting someone of Theo's class to succeed Jim Leighton and it was an extra source of satisfaction that his early performances with Aberdeen contributed to him receiving full international recognition in his native Holland last season.

Theo Snelders . . . the big Dutchman surprised most of us.

I dispute the theory that all goalkeepers are slightly mad otherwise they wouldn't have become goalkeepers in the first place – remember I started off in football as one myself – but it must be admitted that some of the most bizarre stories in the game revolve around that highly individual breed.

My favourite anecdote about Jim Leighton concerns the time the Aberdeen squad were going to Majorca for an end-of-season holiday. Our flight was diverted to Minorca by a severe electrical storm. Accommodation was hastily found for us, but the storm had also affected the electricity supply and when we sat down to our evening meal it was in a hotel dining room lit only by candles.

It was just the kind of atmosphere to suit the telling of ghost stories but Jim took a different tack when, amidst the general conversation around the tables, he caught everyone's attention by announcing that he had an uncle who was a spy in Russia. When we had recovered from the shocked silence which his revelation produced initially, our first question was how he knew his uncle was a spy. After all, it's not something which a secret agent would normally reveal, even to a member of his family. You could hardly imagine this uncle sending Jim a postcard from Moscow: "Wish you were here. Just off to do a spot of spying at the Kremlin" or something like that.

Jim was very young at the time and I think he soon regretted having mentioned his uncle for he was sweating profusely and his hands were shaking as he tried to deal with the torrent of ribald comments and suggestions which his claim provoked from the other players. We didn't uncover any further information on this mysterious relation, but the incident did lead to Jim's existing nickname of "Bozo" being extended to "Bozo Bond" and his appearance at any time during that holiday was the cue for everyone to start humming the theme music from the James Bond film *From Russia With Love*. To this day, however, I often wonder who was pulling whose leg.

CHAPTER FOURTEEN

Pittodrie Profiles

HAVING read in the last chapter that Jim Leighton's original nickname at Pittodrie was Bozo, you might be wondering how on earth he came by it. Well, I'm afraid I cannot enlighten you, but it's a virtual certainty that he was given it by Stuart Kennedy. Stuart was one of those characters that no dressing-room should be without. Involved in everything connected with the club and rarely at a loss for a word or two – or three – he kept everyone's spirits up and eased moments of tension with his ready wit.

An outstanding example of this was the story Alex McLeish quoted in his autobiography. It is, I think, worthy of repetition. Criticised by Alex Ferguson for what the manager described as his "pathetic" crossing of the ball, Stuart claimed he had been working on that aspect of his game and when he appealed to Archie Knox for confirmation, the assistant manager conceded that there had been an improvement. "Oh, you mean I've improved to pathetic?" asked Stuart.

The victim of many of Stuart's wisecracks, strangely enough, was one of his best friends among the players, John McMaster. This was possibly because Johnny's placid, friendly nature fitted him admirably for the role of straight man and he took the ribbing from Stuart in good part.

Stuart Kennedy up to his tricks again as he joins me in an attempt to turn Joe Harper into the abominable snowman. Actually, we are celebrating the news that all three of us are included in the Scotland squad.

Johnny liked to be very fashionable in his dress, but he somehow never quite achieved a direct hit. He was either just ahead or just behind the fashion of the moment. I remember him turning up one day wearing an eye-catching pair of white shoes of a distinctive design. As soon as he entered the dressing-room, Stuart was on the alert. "What's that you've got on your feet?" he asked, and when Johnny admitted they were a recent purchase, Stuart applied the dampener: "They remind me of a pair of bobsleighs." To anyone but a close friend, that could have been a cruel comment, but Johnny was happy that his striking footwear had been noticed.

As I mentioned earlier, Stuart took a keen interest in all the club activities and that included the question of players' bonuses. Whenever a cup final loomed, Stuart was among the first to initiate discussion among the players on what would be a reasonable figure for a winning bonus, and he was able to supply details of what we had been offered on earlier occasions as a basis for negotiation. For these activities, he had the honorary title "The Barrack Room Lawyer" bestowed on him by the club chairman.

Stuart, of course, was not simply an amusing patter merchant. On the field, he was probably one of the best full-backs I have played with. As a defender he was extremely difficult to get the better of, particularly if it was a question of getting around the park. Even in his injury-enforced, premature retirement, it seems that his pace has not deserted him for although I wasn't able to attend Alex McLeish's testimonial match last season, I'm told that Stuart showed up well even against young David Robertson, who is no slouch by any means.

In fact, I can remember only one player whose pace gave Stuart trouble and that was Cha Bum Kun, the South Korean international winger whom we faced against Eintracht Frankfurt in the 1979-80 UEFA Cup. Kun (or should it be Cha?) scored the goal which gave the West German side the lead in the first leg at Pittodrie and we had to depend on an equaliser from Joe Harper to avoid defeat.

In addition to his defensive qualities, Stuart liked to go forward and of the half dozen or so goals he scored in his stay at Pittodrie, the one he is proudest of is undoubtedly the long-range effort which gave us an extra-time victory over Hibs in the League Cup semi-final at Dens Park in December 1978. There was an unkind suggestion that Stuart was intending a cross into the goalmouth, but he insists that he was trying to score, and unless you want a two-hour argument, it's better to accept such an assertion as gospel.

Getting back to nicknames, there is a piece of advice I would like to give to any youngster starting out in professional football. If you have any skeletons in the cupboard, keep them locked away. Give away any secrets to your club-mates and you'll be landed with a nickname which acts as a constant reminder of something you'd probably prefer to forget.

John McMaster, for instance, was known for a spell as "Spammer". This stemmed from a game against Morton at Cappielow, which for Johnny was a trip back to home territory. As he was pointing out his childhood home on the outskirts of Greenock, he let slip that the district used to be known as Spam Valley because the tinned meat which the Americans shipped to us as part of their aid programme during the war was apparently a staple diet in that area. Thereafter he was Spammer.

Less obscure are the origins of some of the other nicknames Aberdeen players have rejoiced in. Neale Cooper's "Tattie" came from a form of rhyming slang. Neale rhymed with peel and peel was associated with tatties, if you see what I mean.

I don't think I have ever come across anyone who, off the field, is as merry as Tattie Cooper. He starts the day with a laugh and finishes it laughing, with lots of laughs in between. He is the kind you always want with you if you have any aspirations as a comedian or storyteller. It can be the most unfunny story in the world but it will still get an appreciative hoot of laughter from Tattie. He's a great character to have in a club and we missed him at Pittodrie for much more than his playing ability when he moved to England, although we weren't altogether happy about his choice of club when he returned north of the border last season to join Rangers.

For all the length of time I've been at Pittodrie, I've never had to endure a nickname for very long myself. Probably the one which stuck longest was "Millet", which arose from a simple misprint of my name in a match programme for one of our European games abroad. The public-address announcer obviously thought nothing strange about reading out Willie Millet as the Aberdeen number six. For a time I was also known as the "Head Waiter", a reference to my preference for playing behind the rest of the defence. It was, I believe, Charlie Nicholas who dubbed me that during his days as a Celtic striker, and I took it as a compliment.

Physical characteristics, of course, are often a ready source of nicknames. I cannot remember calling Gordon Strachan anything other than "Wee Man". Gordon, however, shared with many people of small build a cheeky, bubbling cheerfulness which I'm sure kept him out of possible trouble on a number of occasions. It certainly saved him from my wrath once when we were sharing a hotel room. I couldn't understand why my toothbrush always seemed to be damp when I went to use it until I happened to enter the bathroom to find Gordon scrubbing away at his teeth with my brush. Unperturbed, he explained that he hadn't room in his toilet bag to pack a toothbrush. No wonder! His toilet bag was so tiny that it would have been hard pushed to accommodate a couple of postage stamps – and he didn't think I'd mind him sharing mine. I eventually gave up my protest in disgust, told him to keep my brush, and went out and bought a new one for myself – but I kept it out of sight in case Gordon preferred it to the old one.

At the other end of the physical scale, there was Doug Rougvie. It may have been that his very size was a deterrent, but I can't recall the big Fifer having any particular nickname for long, at least not one we used in his hearing. After we had come across the Rummenigge brothers, Karl-Heinz and Michael, when we met Bayern Munich it was Dougie Rummenigge for a spell, but that was a rather ironic nickname, for skill at the level displayed by the West German brothers was not something Doug Rougvie could rightly claim.

Another tag Doug carried briefly was the Ballingry Bat. He hailed from Ballingry in Fife and the "bat" was a reference to the awe-inspiring image this six-foot-four-inch giant presented with arms and legs outspread as he appealed to the referee after an opponent had tackled him in what he considered an illegal fashion.

For all his outsize physical proportions, Doug was really a gentle soul and I sometimes shudder at the thought of what could have happened to me if he had really taken umbrage when I berated him for some mistake. On occasions I gave him severe stick during a game but he accepted it all meekly with a compliant "yessir".

The squat physical build of Joe Harper was responsible for our ace marksman being known as "Humpty", a contraction of Humpty-Dumpty of nursery rhyme fame. No one, however, worried about Joe's shape as long as he could score goals in the abundance he did. Having set a new club record tally of 173 goals in the course of the hat-trick he claimed in a League Cup-tie against Cowdenbeath at Pittodrie in August 1977, Joe touched the 200 mark with a penalty conversion against Middlesbrough in a pre-season friendly a year later, and he completed his Pittodrie career at the end of season 1980-81 having scored 241 goals in 368 first-team appearances.

Like nearly all prolific scorers, however, Joe suffered those blank periods when the supply of goals just seems to dry up. Early in his first spell with the Dons, he scored 29 goals in 32 games between the start of the 1970-71 season and the end of January, but added only a single goal to that total in 14 appearances in the remaining months of the season.

Whenever Joe got the ball in the opposition's box, you had the feeling that he would score and the only other striker we have had since to give the same feeling was Frank McDougall, whose nickname, incidentally, was Luther. Charlie Nicholas is a bit like that too, but I haven't played long enough with him to be as familiar with his play as I was with Joe's and Frank's.

Apart from great goal-snapping ability, Joe Harper and Frank McDougall had a great deal in common, including the fact that in both cases injury hastened the end of their top-class careers. This may have been coincidence, but it could also be a measure of the extra physical strain to which players who are constantly involved in the hurly-burly of the penalty box are subjected.

Going back to the players who were at Pittodrie in my earlier days there, it was easy to guess why Martin Buchan was known as Elvis. Wherever the Dons travelled, Martin's guitar went too. Very selective in his choice of company, Martin could also have a sharp tongue in his dealings with sections of the Press, as one reporter found out when he asked Martin if he could "have a quick word". "Velocity" came the one-word reply from Martin as he moved on.

There's more of a tale attached to the nickname "Bumper" which Arthur Graham carried for most of his Pittodrie career. It originated apparently from a time when he had one foot in plaster and was getting about on crutches. He didn't, however,

Now you can see why big Doug Rougvie was nicknamed the Ballingry Bat.

let his injury curtail his social activities and he turned up one night at a dance, crutches and all. Arthur couldn't, of course, get his normal shoe on his injured foot, but he had adapted an old training shoe, or "bumper" as it was known, for the purpose.

Dave Robb's desire to be trendy led to him being dubbed Davie Whiteboots at one stage. Someone in England, I think it was Alan Ball, had started off the fashion by appearing in highly distinctive white boots and Davie wouldn't rest until he had acquired a similar pair.

There was one occasion, however, when Davie, individualist that he was, almost had the last laugh on the rest of the players. During one of our trips to Germany, we were to visit the Adidas factory to see their production of soccer gear. Off we went in the team coach, all except Davie Robb, who fancied a visit to the rival Puma factory instead. When we met up again at training, Davie arrived in style in a chauffeur-driven limousine and stepped out fully rigged in new tracksuit and training shoes and carrying a huge bag stuffed with various other items of equipment all supplied free by the factory he had chosen to visit.

Davie's haul of samples compared very favourably with what we had been given – a pair of Adidas Black Samba training shoes – but in his moment of triumph an inglorious downfall awaited. We had hardly started training when Davie tripped and fell flat on his face on the muddy pitch, making a fine mess of his brand new tracksuit.

While on the subject of Pittodrie players of yesteryear, I would like to disagree slightly with the frequently expressed view that Zoltan Varga, the Hungarian exile who had seven months in Scottish football during the 1972-73 season, was the most skilful footballer the Dons have ever had. Without doubt, Zoltan was extremely skilful, with highly developed ball control, but to make that "best ever" assessment is, I feel, not doing full justice to a lot of skilful players we have had at Pittodrie over the years – players who achieved a great deal more for the club than Zoltan did.

Several factors could have contributed to the legend which

has grown up among Aberdeen supporters where Zoltan is concerned, not least of these the general tendency for people and events of years gone by to assume a larger-than-life significance, and for only the good things to be remembered.

In those days, the products of continental football, with its greater concentration on the development of ball skills, were not as numerous on the Scottish scene as they have since become and the novelty of Varga's presence has possibly added lustre to his performance. Then again, his Aberdeen career was comparatively short – he made only 37 first-team appearances, less than half of that number at Pittodrie – so the opportunity to make a balanced judgment in all conditions was limited. Indeed, Zoltan did not look too comfortable or keen to display his talents on some of the frostier days of an Aberdeen winter.

In his brief Aberdeen sojourn, Zoltan certainly made a deep and lasting impression on many of the fans, but it is open to debate whether his silky deftness would have commanded the same appreciation over a longer period. The Scottish fan does look for an element of the physical as well as ball skill in his

It's a fair cop! I get a firm grip on Charlie Nicholas before he can make off with my cheque from a Scottish Brewers monthly award.

Hungarian exile Zoltan Varga signs for Aberdeen in September 1972, as club chairman Dick Donald and manager Jimmy Bonthrone look on.

football. This is demonstrated, I feel, in the experience of players like Robert Connor, Billy Stark, and, to a certain extent, Peter Weir, who have skill in abundance, but are not fully taken to by the crowd because the supporters would prefer to see them get in a few more tackles.

CHAPTER FIFTEEN

Foreign Legions

POSSIBLY the most significant single feature of Scottish football over the last few seasons has been the infusion of fresh blood it has received in players from other countries.

The importation by Scottish clubs of players from overseas is, of course, nothing new – areas such as South Africa, Iceland, the Scandinavian countries and even Australia have for long enough supplied our top clubs with talented individuals – but what was once a mere trickle has now become more of a torrent with the variety of sources greatly widened, particularly on the European continent.

What is new, however, is players coming to Scotland from English clubs – and not just from Third and Fourth Division outfits – in a welcome reversal of the flow which formerly saw a move south of the border regarded as an almost automatic stage in the careers of the cream of Scottish soccer. This development has, of course, been closely associated with the re-emergence of Rangers as a dominating force, which revival, in turn, stems from the appointment of Graeme Souness as manager of the Ibrox club in April 1986.

It is not too difficult to find a cause for the sudden influx of top-class English players. Indeed, it is linked very closely to apparently unrelated phenomena such as Dundee United and Aberdeen each bringing in a number of Scandinavian players in the 1960s and the present Dons' and United management making successful raids on Dutch football. In each of the cases quoted – and there have been other examples – the importations sprang from the Scottish clubs having good contacts in the countries concerned, and this is exactly what happened in Rangers' case.

When Graeme Souness arrived at Ibrox, his knowledge of Scottish club football was rather limited. The market in players of the calibre he wanted was, in any case, restricted in Scotland, and there was the further problem that Rangers would be the last club to whom other leading Scottish clubs would agree to sell players.

It was natural that Graeme should turn his attention to England where he was familiar with the club set-up; knew the people with whom he was dealing; had a wider market to draw on; and where he had in his armoury a potent extra weapon to supplement a ready chequebook. The prospect of playing in the European tourneys, an opportunity which English clubs have been denied since 1985, must have proved a powerful inducement in Rangers' efforts to sign players on the other side of the border.

In criticism of the Rangers' manager's policy, it has been said, with considerable justification, that he hasn't been too selective in his raids on the English player pool, apparently putting more emphasis on quantity rather than quality of players. Graeme, however, was a man in a hurry as he embarked on his campaign to reconstruct the Rangers team and restore the Ibrox club to a challenging force. His premise appears to have been that the wider he spread the net, the greater the chance of finding a valuable fish included in his catch, along with those he could afford to throw back. On that score, his haul has produced some prize catches such as Terry Butcher, Richard Gough and Mark Walters, and quite a number of other captures which have been more than satisfactory. The players who figured regularly in Rangers' treble-winning team of last season included no fewer than seven Englishmen.

The departures from Ibrox of some of Rangers' buys have been as sudden as their arrivals, and after only brief stays, but rarely have the club lost much on the transaction and this has partly offset the mammoth financial outlay involved in such a radical team reconstruction programme.

Whether Rangers have derived full value from their multi-million pound expenditure in winning the Skol Cup three times and the Premier Division twice, is open to debate, with the viewpoint taken depending on where the debater's allegiance lies. I don't suppose many Rangers' supporters would agree with those who contend that, considering the amount of money they have spent, the Ibrox club *should* have swept the boards in domestic competitions for the past three seasons, with possibly a European title thrown in for good measure, but it is an argument which has some merit.

Dramatic as some of the Ibrox earlier captures were, they were tame by comparison with the signing of Mo Johnston in the summer. I'm sure that after the collapse of Mo's proposed return to Celtic, he would have had approaches from a number of other big clubs apart from Rangers and if he had been content to wait a little while longer, he could have found himself a much more comfortable arena in which to display his undoubted football talent.

Leaving aside for a moment the religious question, if that is possible in these particular circumstances, Mo joining Rangers would have, in any case, stirred up controversy in view of his association with the Parkhead club before moving to France, but the apparent renewal of that association and the recriminations resulting from its subsequent breakdown, all coming only a few weeks before his Ibrox arrival, made him a target for extremists on both sides of the religious divide.

Before last season's Celtic-Rangers Scottish Cup final meeting, I tipped Celtic to win, basing that prediction mainly on the fact that they had just signed Mo Johnston. Knowing the Celtic team and supporters as well as I do, I was sure the news of Mo's return would give them a tremendous boost in the final, and so it proved. Imagine, then, the let-down both club and supporters must have suffered when the proposed

Mo Johnston . . . a controversial signing by Graeme Souness.

move turned sour, with salt rubbed in the wound by his almost immediate switch of allegiance to bitter rivals Rangers. Add to this the ingredient of Mo being the Ibrox club's first significant Roman Catholic signing and you have an explosive mixture.

It's not for me to question the rights or wrongs of Mo joining Rangers, but, understanding the depth of the feelings which have been aroused, further polarising opinion in the West of Scotland, I have grave reservations about the wisdom of the move for either the club or the player.

On the playing side, however, the addition of a first-class striker such as Mo Johnston makes Rangers a strong, strong team, for up front was one department, I felt, in which they lacked something, relying too much on Ally McCoist to score goals.

Of the acquisitions Graeme Souness had made in the striking department before Mo, only Kevin Drinkell had made much impact. I think that Graeme – possibly due again to the English influence – was concentrating his search for strikers on players in the big centre-forward mould more commonly found in England rather than on this side of the border where we tend to go for the smaller, quicker kind of striker. That was before Mo Johnston!

Another of the Rangers' manager's aims, I imagine, is an overall reinforcement of his playing pool to avoid being over-dependent on one or two key players. The season before last, for example, was a relatively mediocre one for Rangers with the Skol Cup as their only trophy, and that was put down to being without Terry Butcher for so long with a broken leg. Even last season, the Light Blues struggled for a spell when they didn't have their most consistent scorer, Ally McCoist.

In embarking on a free-spending policy, Rangers have taken a brave gamble and have been single-minded in pursuing it. Several English clubs in the past have tried the same and come close to financial ruin in consequence, but Rangers are possibly one of the few clubs able to sustain such a policy because they are now geared to operating more as a big-business concern than as a football club.

No other club, certainly in Scotland and possibly in Britain, can tap financial resources to the same extent. I don't believe even the Ibrox club themselves could have under their old set-up. The arrival of Graeme Souness and the start of the big spending, however, marked the beginning of the end for the old Rangers and the transformation of a football club into a commercial empire was accelerated when its ownership was taken over by tycoon David Murray last November.

I am no financial expert, but I'd imagine that even a Murray-backed Rangers FC would not find it easy to continue indefinitely laying out cash in the immense sums they have been expending in the last couple of years. The manager's declaration at the end of last season of his intention of working towards a home-reared, all-Scottish team could, in fact, be regarded as the first acknowledgement of recognition that money doesn't come from a bottomless pit, even for Rangers.

In any discussion of Rangers' revival, it is inevitable that sooner or later someone will ask whether having such wide-margin advantages over other clubs in financial terms is good for Scottish football as a whole. In some respects, the question is irrelevant because the answer will almost certainly be coloured by partisanship. How many Rangers' fans would countenance the suggestion that the Ibrox club winning all the domestic honours might be bad for the game in Scotland? Aberdeen or Celtic supporters probably would, but not Rangers! It is the type of question which only someone who is genuinely free of attachment to any Scottish club is likely to answer honestly, and there are not many soccer followers around who are as detached as that. It should not be forgotten that Celtic, Aberdeen – and Rangers themselves – have each enjoyed varying spells of supremacy in the past three decades – and without spending anything approaching Rangers' recent outlay!

Personally, I think Rangers' re-emergence as top dogs last season can be considered harmful to the game only if the other leading clubs in Scotland don't pick up the gauntlet thrown down by the Ibrox club, and find within their own frameworks the means of presenting an effective challenge for the domestic honours.

Anyone who subscribes to the popular myth that the Scots and the English hate each other might imagine that Rangers' Sassenach contingent are given a hard time playing against largely Scottish opposition every week, but I don't suppose they notice much difference from playing in their own country, where they would still be playing alongside and against a fair number of Scots. On the football field, in any case, the popularity of a player is measured on personal qualities – whether he is likeable or otherwise, how good he is at the game – rather than on the accident of his nationality.

I'm not saying that the age-old football rivalry between Scotland and England is not genuine, but for the most part it is an emotion which remains dormant until an international match between the two countries approaches, and is then fanned into life by outside pressures, particularly from the media build-up. Even then, there is little or no animosity between the players of either side. It is rather like an Old Firm game with members of the opposing teams liable to be the best of friends off the field, irrespective of the strong feelings the occasion may arouse among their respective supporters.

I have, for instance, become very friendly with Rangers' skipper Terry Butcher since his arrival at Ibrox as one of the early English imports. I had known him slightly before, but the friendship ripened when our two families found ourselves on the same plane heading for a summer holiday in Florida and we got together several times while we were in the States.

The Butcher and Miller families get together in the sun during a holiday in Florida.

141

The recent increase in players from other countries figuring in Scottish football has given us a valuable foretaste of the day fast approaching when, if the EEC legislators finally have their way, there will be complete freedom of movement for footballers throughout the Community. For the past eight or nine years, the European Union of Football Associations (UEFA) have, understandably, been resisting pressure from the European political body to remove what the politicians see as twin barriers to football's "workers" being able to engage in their occupation freely in any of the Common Market countries. These are (1) the transfer fee system, and (2) restrictions on the number of foreign nationals a club can field.

On the first point, the football authority's argument, and one which seems of late to be getting a more sympathetic hearing from the politicians, is that a transfer fee, or compensation for the loss of a player who wants to move at the end of a contract period, does not interfere with the player's freedom to move. Once he has signed for a new club, it is simply a matter of the two clubs agreeing on a fee, or, in the event of them failing to agree, it being arrived at by the application of a standard formula.

UEFA also argue that the restriction on the number of foreign players allowed – a system which is enforced only in some countries – is purely a football regulation, aimed at safeguarding the interests of the young home nationals of the country concerned. A similar type of restriction now operates in the three European club cup tournaments with teams not allowed to include more than four foreign nationals in these events. Until the 1991-92 season, however, there is a concession for any foreign players signed before 3 May 1988.

The introduction of this rule has extra significance for Scottish clubs in view of the recent increase in imported players, particularly as, in this context, players from other countries in the United Kingdom are regarded as "foreign" in Scotland. This is an interpretation we can hardly quarrel with as long as we insist that the four home countries are separate entities as far as international football is concerned.

The UEFA officials have until 1992 to win the EEC round to their way of thinking, but, in the meantime, even the possibility of transfer fees being abolished is causing concern among club officials in Scotland. That is not surprising for similar alarm bells have been set off by each of the various stages in the emancipation of the professional footballer from the days when he was virtually a victim of slave labour to the more enlightened present in which he enjoys greatly improved terms of employment. In my early days, players signing a new contract were held to ransom over a matter of an extra tenner a week.

Despite all the moans, groans, and lamentations that football couldn't possibly survive all these changes, the game is still with us, and apparently thriving. I wonder how much the introduction of freedom of contract has contributed to that healthy state?

The changes have certainly been beneficial for the players, and, in the long run, I think the clubs have benefited too. Generally speaking, players are quite sensible in negotiating new contracts and they are well aware of what a particular club can or cannot afford in the way of improved terms.

Higher wages are not the only thing players are interested in during these negotiations. If they see that a club is ambitious enough to be prepared to spend a little more money to bring success, they will want to stay there to share in that success.

The reduction in the degree of control over their players which the clubs have suffered through freedom of contract can be partly offset by putting players under longer contracts, thus giving them more security. This, of course, can be taken to unnecessary extremes. I remember when Bristol City were showing an interest in signing me, they were prepared to offer a ten-year contract, which was a bit over the top.

If the abolition of transfer fees does come about in 1992, it will certainly cut off a considerable source of revenue for some clubs, but that could have a beneficial effect in forcing them to develop other sources, such as sponsorship, which they might have neglected as long as they could count on money from transfers.

I can speak with a measure of detachment on the subject of transfer fees as even under the current system I could move to another club at the end of my contract without any transfer fee being involved because I am past the age cut-off point of 33. It seems to me as a player, however, that the removal of transfer fees would be good for my fellow-players while not too harmful to the major clubs. I admit it might be a more severe handicap for the smaller clubs and it could be that special provision will have to be made for them to be recompensed in some way for the loss of players to their big brothers within the same country.

CHAPTER SIXTEEN

Hobby Horses

IN THE course of my career as a professional footballer, I have formed opinions on a great many aspects of the game in Scotland. Most of these views I have kept to myself, partly because officialdom does not always take kindly to players making public pronouncements and has been known to exact retribution under the blanket charge "bringing the game into disrepute", but mainly because no-one has ever asked me for them.

If you have read this far, you'll have already found out what I think on a variety of topics, but there are one or two – rather more, actually – particular areas of Scottish football in which I would like to see changes made, so this chapter is going to be devoted to a selection of my hobby horses, or the bees in my bonnet, if you like.

Take, for example, the number of games we have to play in domestic football in the course of a season. I don't think there is another major footballing country in the world where the fixture list is as congested as it is in either Scotland or England. I am by no means the first to make this point. It has been the complaint of many students of the game for years now, but precious little has been done to curtail the League fixture lists, and the changes that have been made have been cosmetic rather than serious attempts to tackle the problem.

Possibly this has been because the legislators are, for the most part, club representatives and fewer games might mean an overall reduction in gate receipts. I say "might" because it could be argued that given a more restricted choice of games the paying public might turn out in greater numbers at the games which were available.

In fairness to the football authorities, it must be admitted that there have been moves in recent years to slim down the cup competitions. The League Cup showed the way with first a move from its original and rather tedious format of mini-league sections as a preliminary to the knockout stages to a knockout competition with the early rounds being decided on a two-leg, home and away, basis. More recently, as a sponsored event, the Skol Cup, it became a straight knockout tourna-ment and despite fears that it would suffer from the change in character, its short-sharp nature has proved more popular than ever with the fans.

Then there is the Scottish Cup which this season becomes more of a sudden-death affair with drawn ties being permit-ted only one replay. Aberdeen's Scottish Cup meetings with Dundee United in the last two seasons, requiring three games to reach a decision in each case, provided extreme examples of protracted cup-ties which could prejudice the League chal-lenges of each club.

I admit that pruning the League fixture list presents more in the way of practical problems than a similar exercise in the cup competitions, the main obstacle being the wide gap that exists in financial resources, ground facilities, playing stand-ards, and, above all, attitudes to the game, between the big full-time clubs and the smaller part-time outfits.

Since a radical re-think of the Scottish League set-up in the mid-70s produced a Premier Division of ten clubs with the remaining 28 League members split into two divisions, there have been minor adjustments to that format, with varying degrees of success. I believe the present format of a ten-club Premier Division with only one club subject to replacement from Division One each season is, in practical terms, probably the nearest we can get to the ideal, but in my view it still has a couple of weaknesses. One of these is that it necessitates 36 League games, whereas I would suggest that this figure should be no more than 30.

At the same time, I think having 12 clubs in the top division might eventually be the answer, provided that sufficient extra clubs would be prepared to commit themselves to full-time football and could guarantee a reasonable level in their attendance figures. This may seem to contradict my earlier point in that it would entail 44 games under the current system, but if each team played the others three instead of four times, it would mean only 33 games – a little closer to my 30-game target. A difficulty here might lie in deciding how to allocate ground advantage fairly in the case of the third game.

The most obvious way of getting close to the 30-game mark, of course, would be to revert to the old system of a 15 or 16-club top division, the teams playing each other only twice, but I'm afraid we just don't have that many clubs in Scotland of suitable quality to make it a viable proposition.

Whether the Premier Division was composed of ten or 12 clubs, I would stick to the "one up, one down" system for promotion and relegation, as the ratio offering middle-of-the-table clubs the degree of security they need to encourage them to approach each game positively. When two clubs were relegated from a ten-club league, it was a case of four or, at most, five clubs fighting for the title and all the rest scrambling to avoid relegation from the outset. The result was that those clubs with title prospects had in more than half their games to contend with opponents obsessed by defence, and who could blame them when survival was the paramount consideration?

Financially, it is a disaster for a full-time club to lose its Premier Division status and full credit must be given to Dunfermline for remaining on a full-time basis when they were relegated after a brief visit to the top division in season 1987-88. Their faith was vindicated when they gained promotion last season, although it was a close-run affair with the outcome hanging on the final fixtures. Even if the Fifers had been pipped by Falkirk, I believe they would have continued their full-time policy, but thankfully they reaped the reward of their enterprise and are back where they should be – in the Premier Division. Dunfermline are a club who can command gates of 10,000 regularly and Fife deserves to be represented in the highest grade.

Although I don't think the American franchise system, whereby clubs are selected for a League on the basis of their drawing power rather than their playing ability, would suit Scottish football, there is no doubt that the size of a club's support is an important factor. Most players would rather play in a near-full stadium than in a half-empty one, even though that usually means a larger volume of vocal support for the opposition. I say that despite the fact that I seem to have become a prime target for our opponents' followers to hurl their abuse at during a game.

That's all part of the game, and I don't really mind. In fact, I suppose I could take it as a back-handed compliment. I must admit, however, that baiting Willie Miller seems to have risen sharply in the ratings for popular pastimes. It wasn't so bad when Alex Ferguson was Aberdeen's manager, for most of the taunts were directed at him, but when Ian Porterfield succeeded Fergie, the opposition's boo-boys didn't know enough about him to single him out for special attention, so they moved on to focus on me.

To return to my beef about there being too many games in domestic competition, I feel that the spectators would find compensation for the loss of games caused by a reduction in being able to watch a higher level of performance from the players. The physical demands of playing 50 to 60 games in a season is something which is not generally considered, or even appreciated, by the spectator, but it makes it difficult to maintain a consistently high standard week in, week out, particularly for midfield players who have to get through a power of work.

Discussing possible changes in the League format like this, of course, raises the question of the ability of the leading clubs to make changes as circumstances demand. At one time, the big clubs, for all their superiority in wealth, were very much at the mercy of their lesser brethren, who by sheer weight of numbers in voting could effectively strangle at birth any proposals which did not have their approval, but there have been signs that the Premier clubs can have their way if they are determined enough and united in pursuit of their objective.

I think the time is bound to come when the leading clubs have a greater degree of control over their own destinies. This is especially important in matters such as discussions with potential sponsors and the formulation of television agreements. There is big money involved in these deals and it is the glamour clubs who are principally concerned because their games are what the sponsors or television companies are seeking to use.

Possibly the best way of rationalising the Scottish football set-up to ensure that the full-time clubs' particular needs are met would be, as has already been mooted, to amalgamate the SFA and the Scottish League into one body. This would cut down on administration costs and provide an umbrella under which separate committees could handle the affairs of the various divisions. Provision could also be made for the Scottish Professional Footballers' Association – the Players' Union, as it is often known – to be represented on this single national body. As things stand at the moment, the biggest problem the SPFA faces in the welfare area of its operations is that it is sadly under-funded. If it were to be given a say in the national football association, the build-up of the large pension fund it needs might be easier. An obvious source of money for this purpose would be a small percentage levied on each transfer fee paid, as happens in some countries. This method of raising funds, however, might not have much future if the transfer fee system is going to be scrapped in a few years.

All that, however, is in the future. Returning to the present, the Premier Division certainly has a product to sell, and I would go as far as saying that we have overtaken our English counterparts in this respect. Across the border they have always claimed that they have the best league in the world. They still make that claim, but it now has a rather hollow ring to it.

It is not only on the quality of football that these judgments are made. The fans, too, have an important part to play in the overall picture which is projected. I would like to think that Aberdeen and Dundee United have in recent years made major contributions to raising the standing of Scottish football in the eyes of Europe in terms of both quality of play and the conduct of their supporters. United and ourselves, between us, have produced a number of sustained runs in Europe and this, together with our fans' impressive behaviour on these occasions, has done much to banish any reservations the continentals may have had previously about Scottish football.

You might ask if it matters very much what people abroad think about our football, but consider how England's reputation has slumped to an all-time low through the repeated misbehaviour of English supporters. That kind of malaise can have an effect on footballing standards, and I believe this is happening in England, where the game is also suffering through lack of games against continental clubs – the consequence of their fans' misbehaviour!

The Dons' and United's European showing has also served to rid followers of football on the continent of the idea many of them had that the only two clubs of any significance in Scotland are Rangers and Celtic. Before our European Cup-Winners' Cup win in 1983, I cannot recall ever getting a letter from Europe asking for a photograph, but such a request has been a fairly common occurrence since. On a personal level, that is an indication of what Scottish club football being recognised abroad means.

Overall, however, Scotland's international record is a strange mixture of brilliance and mediocrity. It is probably this very unpredictable quality which causes even the best soccer nations some apprehension about facing us.

As fans, too, we have our highs and lows, carried away by only moderate success at one time, over-critical of the national team at another. The euphoria leading up to the 1978 World Cup finals in Argentina was an extreme example of the first of these tendencies, and the gloom which followed that disaster was all the deeper for regret over our earlier foolishness. I doubt whether the lessons of 1978 have been fully absorbed by all Scotland followers, but Jock Stein certainly did his best to instil a more realistic level of expectation into the fans. He always tended to underplay our prospects before a game and he did it so consistently that I'm sure it was a deliberate policy on his part.

There is, however, still an arrogance about the Scottish fans and it irritates me that through ignorance of the standards of football which currently prevail among the so-called "rabbits" of the soccer world, both the public and the media in Scotland assume that these countries' teams are there for the beating – and expect Scotland to beat them handsomely! I'm sure many of the regular attenders at the Aberdeen International Football Festival have been surprised by the degree of skill shown by the Nigerian teams who have appeared in the festival. The same kind of advances are being made in football outposts all over the world, and at all age levels. The sooner we understand that, the better.

We could take the matter a stage farther and ask ourselves how these comparatively new football nations have made so much progress so quickly. In most cases, at least part of the answer lies in modern coaching methods. In these countries, of course, they have the advantage of starting from scratch when the basics can be instilled without bad habits having to be unlearned first, as is the case in countries such as ours which have a longer football history.

There is also a tendency in Scotland for the older generation to be suspicious of coaching – could this be another manifestation of Scottish arrogance in football matters – a "football is our game, we don't need coaching" kind of attitude? It is often claimed that Scottish football is spoiled by over-coaching. I don't believe this is the case and I don't think many other senior players would agree with the over-coaching theory either. Those who put it forward – in many cases former footballers turned commentators on the game – are, for the most part, people who have never been coached themselves and don't really know what it's all about because in their day it simply didn't exist.

Basically, there is not as much natural football talent in Scotland as there used to be, because the changing environment and social habits mean that children no longer play football in the streets from morning to night for lack of anything better to occupy their time. What natural talent there is, however, must be developed as early as possible and proper coaching is the way to do that.

Certainly, there are good coaches and bad coaches, and the aim of the SFA coaching courses is to ensure that there are more good than bad by making sound coaching methods available. What each person attending such a course takes from it depends entirely, of course, on the person himself, but the more courses he attends, the more bits and pieces he has to choose from in building his own coaching method. Probably the most important function of the coaching course is imparting to the coach the ability to communicate with his charges so that the experience he gains can be passed on in a form which will benefit those receiving the coaching.

My comment about there being good and bad coaches applies equally to another group of people who are increasingly looming large on the soccer scene – players' agents. You can sometimes tell if someone in football is a player or a manager by the tone of his voice when he utters the word agent, such is the division of views on these gentlemen.

If I ever become a manager, I'll probably share in the general antipathy which club bosses have for agents, although by that time the role of the agent may well have changed radically. Speaking from my present position as a senior player, however, I think there *is* a place in the game for someone to represent the individual player, negotiating deals on his behalf, and acting as an intermediary between player and club. In everyday life, individuals or business concerns have lawyers to look after their interests and guide them through the legal maze of a contract. Why should football be different?

I think players' agents in this country might gain more respectability if, as happens elsewhere, they had to be registered as such, and had to meet certain criteria in qualification before they could obtain official accreditation. Then a player could go to an agent knowing that his credentials had been scrutinised by the football authorities or possibly by the Players' Union before he was permitted to operate. That would afford the player some protection against the con-man.

Agents are a relatively recent development in the game and were practically unheard of in my younger days, but if I were a 21-year-old all over again, I would get myself an agent. Not so much to negotiate with a club on my behalf, but more to ensure that I was getting the best deal possible. The agent has more freedom to tap the interest of clubs in Europe and farther afield. That may sound mercenary, but a professional footballer's career is all too short and he owes it to his family to make provision for the time when he no longer has the same high earning capacity.

The importance of coaching is that the coaches themselves are properly instructed ... SFA director of coaching Andy Roxburgh, assisted by former Montrose manager Kenny Cameron, conducts a course for youth coaches in the north-east.

Earlier in this chapter, I commented on the tendency of the Scottish media, in common with the football public, to underestimate some of the newer footballing countries simply because they are not sufficiently well-informed about the standards that have been reached in these countries. That situation is rapidly improving, for with the arrival of cable TV, football followers in this country are now getting more opportunity to see matches abroad more regularly and appreciate how the game is played in other countries, while last summer's Under-16 World Cup finals in Scotland must also have opened the eyes of fans here to the fact that these so-called under-developed countries can play a bit.

This, however, is not the only aspect of Scottish press, radio and TV reporting of football which often saddens, and, at times, angers me. I know the media has an important and influential role in football, stimulating and maintaining public interest in the game, but I wish some sections of our sporting press would take a more responsible attitude to their obligations.

I'm referring, of course, principally to the more sensational tabloid newspapers who seem too intent on producing an eye-catching headline and an "exclusive" tag to give much consideration to the accuracy or otherwise of the story.

I can understand that when newspapers are involved in a circulation war, the reporter finds himself at the sharp end of the campaign, under pressure from his Sports Desk to get a "better" story than the rival paper. Understanding how it comes about that comments made in good faith are misquoted and facts distorted does not, however, make the final product any more acceptable to the poor victim.

The saddest thing is that the newspapers who pay least attention to accuracy are almost invariably the ones that are most widely read. I recall seeing a television programme surveying newspaper readers. About 90% of those interviewed said they didn't believe most of what they read in the tabloids but they still enjoyed reading them! – a sad commentary on the people who buy these papers.

The fact the most of the papers' readers do not believe

what they are reading may be of some comfort to the person maligned, but you would have to have the skin of a rhinoceros not to be hurt by some of the stories which appear. I try to forget it, but I still feel bitter when I recall one occasion when I was labelled "a con-man and a cheat". I can't even remember the incident which occasioned this description or why I was singled out for it, but it was probably another example of me having taken over from Alex Ferguson as principal target for anyone wishing to vilify the Aberdeen club. Not all the adverse comments, of course, are as hurtful as that one. Most of them are mere pinpricks which are felt only if repeated time and again.

In Chapter Six I recalled an incident early in my international career when I was criticised for missing a scoring chance by a television commentator, who conveniently overlooked similar lapses by other members of the side who were recognised as goal scorers. Some players can avoid criticism by "going missing" for long spells in a game, escaping the observer's notice by remaining largely anonymous, while others pay an unfair penalty for always trying to be positive. Kenny Dalglish, for example, was frequently slated for his international performances because, no matter how he was playing, he was always in the thick of the action trying to contribute to the team effort. Consequently, when it did not come off for him, his failure was all the more noticeable.

I don't think it is as prevalent now, but at one time sections of the Scottish Press, possibly through acceptance of the fallacy, promoted by their English counterparts, that the English League was the best in the world, seemed to be convinced that no-one was worthy of a place in the Scotland team unless he was either an Anglo-Scot or he played for Rangers or Celtic.

The first time I felt that players such as Alex McLeish and myself had been fully accepted as international candidates by the Press on both sides of the border was after the England-Scotland game at Wembley in 1981, which, as you may recall, Scotland won thanks to a John Robertson penalty. Alex and I had had a good game, handling the combined talents of Peter

Withe, Tony Woodcock and Trevor Francis – who were then at their peak – effectively, but the attention I received from the Press after the game came as a complete surprise. Certainly, I was happy with my performance in that game, but there had been earlier occasions when I felt I had played just as well, or perhaps even better, without all this fuss being made.

While I cannot approve of the methods some of our national newspapers are adopting, presumably prompted by the cut-throat battle for circulation, I am happy to say that I am on reasonably good terms with most of the people who have to supply the stories for their sports pages. There are some I steer clear of, but in general they're OK if you make allowance for the professional pressures they are operating under.

CHAPTER SEVENTEEN

Good for a Laugh

I'M SURE you've heard it whenever football is being discussed. One of the older generation is almost bound to bemoan the absence of "characters" in the game today. From the spectator's point of view, there is probably a lot of truth in the comment. The demands of modern-day professional football are such that players have to conform to a team pattern to some degree and there is less scope for the individualist to express himself. In this context, it's interesting to speculate on how a Charlie Tully or a Jim Baxter would fare in present-day football.

This admission, however, does not mean that the football of today is without its share of characters. It's just, I think, that for the most part it's off the field of play that they are to be found. It may be outwith the public sight or knowledge that they flourish, but the contribution they make to a team's performance is nevertheless of immense value.

On the international front, my nomination for character par excellence would be Jimmy Steel. "Jimmy who?" you might ask. Well, Steelie, as he is universally known in football circles, is officially masseur to both Celtic and Scotland squads, a double function he has fulfilled for many years and continues to do

Jimmy Steel and Alan Rough . . . entertaining characters.

so despite a recent illness and being long past retirement age. Effective as his hands are in relaxing muscles, Steelie's greatest gifts lie in relaxation in a wider sense, his superb mimicry and impish humour having eased away tension from a succession of club and international squads over the years.

The few hours before a big game can be a nerve-racking time for the players, particularly the less experienced ones, but Steelie is just the man to ease the ordeal by taking their minds off the game ahead. On the coach travelling to, say, Wembley, he will take over the microphone and give an hilarious running commentary of an imaginary boxing match – he was at one time involved in professional boxing as a masseur and knew many of the top fighters.

Alan Rough is an entertaining character with a quieter, almost confidential, approach, but he too loves an audience. When I first joined the group usually surrounding the 'keeper, I was impressed with the fluency with which he related a series of humorous stories, all of them new to me. It was some time before I began to realise that I had heard this or that story before. He had such a huge repertoire that he could go on for long enough, but if you were in his audience often enough, you discovered that it did have its limits and that Roughie was beginning to repeat himself. Not that that mattered too much because the composition of his audience had usually changed considerably by that time.

For Partick Thistle and Scotland Under-23 trainer Donnie MacKinnon, audience participation was an essential part of two tricks in which he specialised. One of these involved showing a newcomer to the squad how to keep a coin on his forehead with his head in an upright position. Donnie would demonstrate by wetting one side of the coin and placing it in the middle of his forehead where it might stick for a count of perhaps four or five. Then he would do the same for his guinea pig except that in the course of applying the coin to his victim's forehead, he would deftly remove it in the same motion. The primed audience would then start counting and with growing excitement as the count mounted into double figures while the victim waited for the penny to drop, in more senses than one. Sometimes it needed the production of a mirror to convince him that the coin was not still stuck to his forehead.

Donnie's other speciality was even more mystifying and involved telephone communication with the all-knowing Phantom. It was a long time before any of us discovered how this one was worked.

The victim was asked to select any playing card from an ordinary pack and show it to the rest of the company. Donnie then dialled the Phantom's number – no-one else was allowed to make the connection – but it was invariably a bad line and he would utter a series of "hellos" interspersed with remarks like, "Is that the Phantom?" These were really pre-arranged signals for at the other end of the telephone line, the Phantom was listing the suits: "Hearts, Diamonds, Clubs, Spades", with Donnie's "Hello" indicating the right suit. Then the Phantom would go through the cards of that suit from ace to king until he was interrupted at the appropriate point by Donnie's next "Hello". The climax came when Donnie had apparently established satisfactory contact and the receiver was passed to the victim, to be informed by the Phantom's voice that he had selected such and such a card.

As I mentioned, it took a long time for us to twig how this trick worked, and even longer to discover that the Phantom was really former international Ronnie Glavin. Donnie and Ronnie had cooked up the trick when they were both with Partick Thistle, and after that Ronnie could expect a phone call from anywhere in the world a Scotland squad happened to be.

There was, however, one occasion when I was less than amused by Donnie MacKinnon. It was during the 1981 England-Scotland game at Wembley which I referred to in the last chapter. As we prepared to start the second half, I noticed that Trevor Francis had been substituted for Tony Woodcock in the England line-up, but before play got under way, Donnie, having sprinted 50 yards from the bench, suddenly appeared at my shoulder with whispered instructions: "Watch out for Francis, he's like lightning." To be fair, Donnie had probably been despatched by Jock Stein, but I was irritated by the suggestion that I might fail to notice a change in my direct opposition and know what to expect of the new player.

The Aberdeen club has had its share of "characters" over the years, some of whom I have mentioned in other contexts in earlier chapters. On the management side, Alex Ferguson and Archie Knox would both qualify for the description, each different from the other in some respects, so alike in others. Archie's booming voice may not endear him to everyone, but it was perfectly suited for handling a group of noisy youngsters. A non-stop worker, Archie lives and breathes football, with everything else coming second. Fergie is known for his volatility and I have often wondered how much his abrupt changes of mood were contrived to underline a point. I have even heard it suggested that he would punch a door or something equally hard before entering the dressing-room after a bad game to ensure that he was really angry in dealing with his wayward players. The pain would have worn off by the time he had ended his tirade and he could leave the dressing-room calm once more.

Then there is Teddy Scott, whose chief qualification as a "character" lies in his utter and almost unique reliability. The quiet, thoughtful, ever-present, ever-helpful Ted, as ready to give you the benefit of his accumulated wisdom when asked for it as he is to ensure that you have the right gear awaiting you for either a game or a training session.

On the playing side at Pittodrie, I have already related some anecdotes which show players such as Stuart Kennedy and Doug Rougvie as individualists, but one of my favourite memories of the latter is his ability to handle hostile opposition supporters. When visiting Parkhead, most of us go out for the pre-match warm-up with some trepidation, knowing the kind of reception we can expect from the Celtic fans. Big Doug, however, used to make a point of working out on his own on the touchline right in front of the Jungle, acknowledging the insults hurled in his direction with a charming smile and a cheery wave. Only he could get away with that! Whoever Doug plays for, his relationship with his club's fans is something

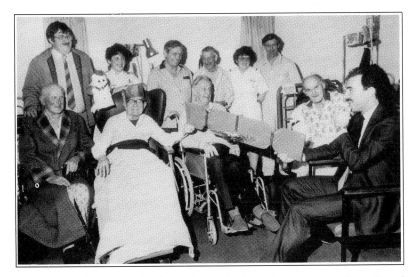

Meeting the fans . . . sharing a laugh with patients at Aberdeen Royal Infirmary.

161

special and it was good to see him returning to the Scottish scene this season. Signing for Dunfermline must have been a real homecoming for the big Fifer.

Doug also figures in one of my recollections of the Dons' Far East tour in the summer of 1974. When we gathered at the airport to set out on that adventure, Doug was accompanied by the largest suitcase I have ever seen. It was totally in keeping with his own outsize proportions.

Speaking of the 1974 tour reminds me of the misfortune which befell Willie Young through "counting his chickens". On our way home from Australia and New Zealand, we stopped over in Hong Kong and nearly everyone in the party took advantage of the opportunity to buy a watch at duty-free prices. Willie, however, decided that this was too good a bargain to miss and he bought watches for all his relations and stowed them in different parts of his luggage, hoping they would escape the attention of the Customs at Heathrow. His hopes seemed to be fulfilled when he passed through the barrier without being challenged, but he couldn't resist communicating his good luck to the rest of us, and in a loud voice. Willie's glee was short-lived, however, for he was approached by a Customs officer and asked to return to the barrier where his illicit goods were uncovered. We had been in our London hotel for a couple of hours before we were finally joined by a disconsolate Willie with his Customs dues settled.

The stories told about the late Bobby Calder are legion, and even before the start of my Pittodrie career, he was the first "character" connected with the Aberdeen club I came across. The Dons' chief scout was at that time probably more widely known in Glasgow than he was in Aberdeen.

I remember being in a group of youngsters travelling north to Pittodrie under Bobby's care when he revealed the secret of a scar which he carried on his forehead. His story was that while refereeing a match in South America, someone in the crowd fired a gun at him. According to Bobby, he saw the bullet coming and almost, but not quite, got out of its way. That he should be fired on from the crowd may be believable, but the rest of the story must be taken with a pinch of salt. Hearing it, however, as a naïve 16-year-old, I probably swallowed it whole!

Some of the most entertaining times I have had during my Pittodrie career have been in evenings spent in the company of Aberdeen supporters. At one time or another, I must have visited every one of the branches spread over a wide area of the Scottish mainland and the islands, and I have found them great hosts with some real "characters" among their members.

Avoiding one of their practices, however, has called for a bit of diplomacy on my part. When a player is visiting one of the supporters' club functions, usually to receive an award, it is quite common for the evening to end with the guest of honour being carried round the hall shoulder-high by some of the younger and lustier members. This was something I found acutely embarrassing and I devised a way round the problem by making a tactical early withdrawal from the function just before the finale. The secret lies in judging the right moment to say farewell.

CHAPTER EIGHTEEN

Pick of the Crop

WITH all due respect to the football writers and other bodies who present players' merit awards, there is something special about being chosen for such an award by one's fellow professionals. No matter how closely, or knowledgeably, a spectator studies a game, the judges best qualified to assess how good a particular player is are those playing alongside or against him. Not only do they have a better vantage point, but they probably also reach their verdict on more professional criteria.

These observations may be less than profound, but they serve as an appropriate introduction to a chapter in which I would like to recall some of the outstanding players I have been privileged to encounter in my playing career. With a single notable exception, I have, for the reason stated, confined my selection to players I have actually played against.

The list may seem to carry a heavy preponderance of foreign players, but this, I think, can be explained partly by the likelihood that these players made a deeper impression on me meeting them only once or twice than if I were opposing them several times a season for several years, as is the case with the top Scottish-based players, and partly because my range of choice is virtually world-wide and Scotland, whatever our

164

aspirations, is, in world football terms, only one small country.

Not surprisingly, most of the players discussed are, or in some cases were, strikers and this is because they are the opponents I have had most direct experience of and have had the best opportunity to study at close quarters.

The one exception is Diego Maradona and I claim special exemption in his case because I came close to playing against the Argentinian superstar. That was way back in June 1979 when the 18-year-old Maradona, who even then was being acclaimed as crown prince to the soccer throne occupied by Pele, figured prominently in the Argentinian team which beat Scotland 3-1 in a friendly international at Hampden Park.

My chances of making the Scotland team seemed reasonably good when I was called into the squad following the home international series as a heavy crop of withdrawals included a number of defenders in Gordon McQueen, Sandy Jardine, Martin Buchan and Stuart Kennedy. At that time, however, I had only two full caps behind me, while Alan Hansen and Dundee United pair Dave Narey and Paul Hegarty were all available, so I had to content myself with a place on the bench. Even the hope of a substitute appearance faded when George Wood replaced Alan Rough in goal just after the interval and Frank Gray took over from Asa Hartford midway through the second half, leaving me on the bench with Joe Jordan and Willie Wallace.

In some respects I could perhaps count myself fortunate to be watching – and enjoying – Maradona's performance along with the 62,000 Hampden spectators rather than being out there trying to stop him, but on balance I think I would have preferred to accept the challenge of playing against him.

Despite his youth, the chunky Argentinian lived up to the glowing reports we had had of his promise. He created the opening for Argentina's opening goal, scored by Leopoldo Luque, with a run through the middle very similar to the one which brought him a goal against England in the 1986 World Cup finals in Mexico, resisting several challenges en route. After Luque had scored again, Maradona helped himself to

Karl Heinz Rummenigge . . . a hot handful.

a cheeky goal before my former Pittodrie club-mate Arthur Graham scored Scotland's consolation counter.

Even as a teenager Maradona had remarkable skill and control, and, most significantly, the superb balance which enabled him to ride the best of tackles and still keep possession of the ball. Since then he has made his name known throughout the football world as a worthy successor to fellow South American

Pele, whom we all put on a pedestal as school kids. I sometimes wonder, however, if Maradona has fully realised his early potential. It's a hypothetical question, I know, but could he have been an even better footballer if he had remained in his native country instead of falling for the lure of the fleshpots of Italian football, and its consequent glare of publicity?

Topping the list of strikers I have had to cope with personally would probably be Karl-Heinz Rummenigge, and I'm proud that the West German, who was then rated one of the best strikers in the world, was not allowed to shine on the two occasions we met when Aberdeen beat Bayern Munich in the quarter-final of the European Cup-Winners' Cup in 1983.

Appreciating the danger he represented, I had studied his play, and knew in advance how I wanted to deal with him. The two golden rules I had decided on were to remain on my feet and to resist the temptation to dive into the tackle. Rummenigge was the kind of player who invited such a challenge and then took advantage of the opponent being off balance to go round him. Only once over the two legs did I forget my rules and as soon as I had committed myself I knew I had made a mistake. Sure enough, he went past me, but fortunately Jim Leighton saved my blushes with a good save.

Rummenigge's striking partner when we played Bayern was Dieter Hoeness, brother of the more famous Ulli, and he and Rummenigge made an effective pairing. If I were looking for a striker to complement Karl-Heinz, however, I would go for Real Madrid's Emil Butragueno.

The Spaniard is the kind of attacker who can't be marked by one player because he wanders about all over the place. You have to depend on all the defenders looking after him when he appears in their area. Like Maradona, he has that fine sense of balance which makes him difficult to dispossess, but, unlike the Argentinian, he does not enjoy as much acclaim as I think he deserves. It was therefore of great satisfaction to me that Butragueno was kept well under control when Scotland shared a goalless draw with Spain in a friendly in Madrid's Bernabeu Stadium in April 1988. Alex McLeish was in particularly good form that night and between us we kept Butragueno quiet.

Actually, the striker who gave me the most uncomfortable 45 minutes in a European tie was Walter Schachner of Austria Memphis, whom we ousted from the first round of the European Cup in 1980. In the first leg at Pittodrie, we reached the interval with a one-goal lead, thanks to Mark McGhee snatching what proved the only goal of the 180 minutes, but that interval scoreline was something of a travesty for we had been given a real roasting by the Austrians in the first half.

Adopting what was later to become recognised as our standard European tactics, we pushed up to pressurise the visitors, but the Austrians merely lobbed long balls over the defenders' heads for Schachner to chase, which he did with an unbelievable turn of speed. Fortunately for us, Schachner's finishing on that occasion did not match his leading-up work and he missed several chances created by his electrifying pace.

As the half progressed, I realised that we were going to have to re-think our tactics, so I dropped back to a deeper – much deeper – position and also warned full-backs Stuart Kennedy and Doug Rougvie about narrowing their operational areas as a further precaution. The changes gave us a slightly more comfortable second half and Schachner did not pose as many problems in the goalless second leg in Vienna.

Although that was our first appearance in the Champions' Cup, it wasn't our first experience of coming up against a speed merchant in a European tie – and it wasn't our last either as most Continental teams seemed to have at least one pacey player. A season earlier, our UEFA Cup opponents, Eintracht Frankfurt, had such a player in South Korean international Cha Bum Kun. I have mentioned in an earlier chapter how he could show even Stuart Kennedy a clean pair of heels.

Pace was also a potent weapon for Michael Laudrup, who set up a formidable striking partnership with Preben Elkjaer for Denmark in the World Cup finals in Mexico. Laudrup was the deeper-lying of the two, but he was just as dangerous as his partner, although it was Elkjaer who probably caught the eye more as the leader of the attack. When he did go, however, Laudrup was hard to catch and I must admit that I had to resort to tripping him on one occasion when he caught me off balance. I justified the foul to myself as being in the national interest.

Dealing with the calibre of strikers I have mentioned, the defender needs to give them only one chance, or even a half-chance sometimes, and it can be enough to lose a game. In Scotland, we don't somehow seem to be able to breed attackers who possess both skill and pace to such a high degree. We have had front men of great skill like Kenny Dalglish and Denis Law, to mention only a couple, but none of them particularly noted for pace. That, in fact, was probably the only deficiency in Kenny Dalglish's game. Speed is something which can be improved with hard work in training, but basically it is a gift, and one with which we Scots don't seem to be richly endowed.

Speaking as a defender, I have had ample first-hand opportunity to appreciate the problems of playing against these speed merchants, but they can be countered if you use your head. You don't have to be able to match your opponent for pace providing you have a reasonable positional sense, and can avoid trying to engage him in a straight race.

As indicated elsewhere, I have had skirmishes on the international scene with successive team managers who periodically wanted to employ a squarer defensive system. In my view, you simply can't play like that against pacey strikers without exposing yourself to great risk. All the top footballing countries have proved that by relying on a deep-lying sweeper.

Probably the strongest argument I can put forward in support of my case is Franz Beckenbauer, but that is not the elegant West German defender's only qualification for a mention in this chapter. The Kaiser's superb reading of the play, his timing, his use of the ball and an arrogant self-confidence combined to make him one of the all-time greats of football, and certainly one of my boyhood heroes.

Because of my long-standing admiration for Beckenbauer, it proved something of a disappointment when I actually played against him in Aberdeen's UEFA Cup third-round clash with SV Hamburg in 1981. By that time, Beckenbauer was 36 and past his peak. It was also a November night for the first leg at Pittodrie and a light covering of snow on the pitch made ground conditions far from ideal for control of either the ball or one's feet, while our policy of pressurising European opponents did not allow him the time on the ball he was accustomed to. (I wonder how he would have fared in the hurly-burly of Premier Division football?)

All these factors contributed to Beckenbauer not being too prominent as Aberdeen took a 3-2 first-leg lead which should have been much more emphatic. We lost two silly goals, the second a late one, after Doug Rougvie had been injured and before Neale Cooper took his place, while Gordon Strachan failed from the penalty spot earlier in the game. We paid for these lapses with a 3-1 defeat in the second leg in Hamburg to lose on a 5-4 aggregate.

While Franz Beckenbauer was not at his best in these games, he still gave glimpses of his class. Apart from sharing a liking for playing deep, he and I are too dissimilar in physique and playing style for me to model my game on that of the West German star, but I did pick up one or two useful pointers from watching him, particularly his great positional sense.

Aberdeen's meetings with SV Hamburg then and in the Super Cup two years later brought us up against an outstanding midfield player in Felix Magath. Remembering that at international level the midfield men I have played against include the likes of Michel Platini, you might wonder why I single out Magath for special mention. Well, much as I admire Platini's play, Magath had a special quality which I consider valuable in a midfield player. In addition to being a first-class all-round player, he had the ability to take control of the midfield department and boss the other players.

Off the field, Magath was, I understand, what our club chairman would describe as a "barrack room lawyer" and I suppose it was this strong-willed independent attitude which contributed to his success as a midfield general, although I have heard it suggested that his haul of international caps might have been greater had he been less prone to question authority. I certainly recall that before Hamburg played the second leg of the Super Cup at Pittodrie in December 1983 there was threat of a players' revolt over some matter of club policy and it wouldn't be surprising if Magath was very much involved in that dispute.

While I think that the midfield of every team should have a dominant player like Magath, I'm not sure whether there's room for more than one player of this type. Having said that, however, Leeds United did not suffer, during their glory years, from having Billy Bremner and Johnny Giles – both bossy players – operating together in midfield.

Speaking about midfield, that was a department in which FC Porto were particularly strong when they beat us in the semi-final of the 1983-84 Cup-Winners' Cup before going on to lose to Juventus in the final. Costa and Sousa are the names which come readily to mind in the Porto midfield but, to be completely frank, the Portuguese players looked so much alike that I found it difficult to distinguish one from another.

Strikers, defenders and midfield men have all figured in this chapter, but no mention so far of goalkeepers. Well, in all honesty, I cannot say that in the teams I have played against I have come across a performer as outstanding in this highly specialised position as the outfield players I have mentioned have been in their positions. There have been in the opposition many very competent keepers and I particularly remember Rinat Dasayev, who showed good control of his goalmouth in the Scotland-Russia game in the 1982 World Cup finals in Spain – he was later judged the best goalkeeper in the finals – but I cannot think of any whom I would rate above the goalkeepers I have had playing behind me such as Bobby Clark, Alan Rough, Jim Leighton and Theo Snelders. What higher compliment can I pay them?

CHAPTER NINETEEN

The Family Pays

PRESSURE is a word which crops up frequently in football circles and in a vocabulary which often pays scant regard to the dictionary definition of words misused daily, it is one that has somehow avoided the fate of becoming a mere cliché. Players and managers alike complain about pressures of varied types and from a variety of sources. They are certainly subject to such forces but, speaking as a player, I reckon we get off lightly in this respect – compared, that is, to our wives and families.

While we are deriving enjoyment from playing a game we love (and would probably be playing even if we were not paid for doing so), they have to withstand pressures which are not immediately apparent to the outsider and which far outweigh any reflected glory a successful footballer's kin might enjoy. The problem is probably even more acute in the case of club managers with former Aberdeen boss Ian Porterfield a recent example of a manager being persuaded to resign at least partly as the result of malicious gossip upsetting his family, but players' families, too, are subject to this.

I am fortunate in that my children, nine-year-old Victoria and five-year-old Mark, are still on the young side for it to be a serious problem, but even very young schoolchildren can be very cruel to their classmates.

As far as the player's wife is concerned, the pressure can be felt in two main areas. One is the curtailment which professional football imposes on social life. Although the full-time footballer generally has considerable free time to spend with his family at times when he would not be available if he had a

The Miller family; wife Claire, Mark (5) and Victoria (9).

regular nine to five, Monday to Friday job, he has to pay for this by frequent absences from home – and mostly at weekends when the level of social activity is highest.

Friday evening, which most people regard as a social occasion, is ruled out as such for the professional footballer during the season whether he is playing at home or away the following day. Then there are European trips which involve three or four-day midweek absences, while the same applies for international calls, with the absences considerably longer in the case of World Cup finals. I have been in the Scotland squad for two of these, as well as travelling to join international squads on over 100 other occasions. Although there has not always been a game for me on these trips, they have, on the whole, been enjoyable experiences while my wife Claire was left at home to handle domestic and family affairs single-handed in my absence, having to depend on friends for baby-sitting duties as she has no immediate relations in the Aberdeen area.

The second form in which pressure manifests itself is the degree of attention which a prominent footballer can receive from the media, and in this the children can be affected as much as the wife. Adverse publicity is something which most professional footballers experience at some time or other and usually they learn by experience how to handle it, but it is often harder for their families to bear.

Scotland assistant manager Craig Brown tells a story which illustrates this point.

When the national squad are together preparing for a match, training sessions usually end with a practice game and sometimes it is difficult to find a natural division for splitting the squad into two sides. Obvious ones such as Home Scots v. Anglos and club combinations are not always appropriate for an even division, so something a little more bizarre is called for. On this particular occasion it was Ugly Guys against the Good Lookers – no prizes for guessing which side was allocated my mates Jim Leighton, with his bandy legs, and Alex McLeish, with his squint nose. Anyway, it came down to Murdo MacLeod as the last player and he landed in the Ugly Squad – without any protest on his part. The Celtic

Claire contributes to the business enterprises, recording a voice-over for a commercial.

(as he was then) player, however, apparently mentioned the incident in a phone call to his wife and as Craig Brown was leaving Glasgow Airport after the homeward flight, he was button-holed by an irate Mrs MacLeod, accompanied by two small children. Murdo's wife wanted to know why her husband had been allocated to the Ugly Guys team, and the youngsters chipped in loyally with "My Daddy should have been in the Good Looking team." Exit a chastened Mr Brown!

Some football wives react quite strongly to hearing their husbands criticised in public. Claire, for example, has been known to take issue with fans who castigate me unfairly in her hearing while she is watching a game, and from what I'm told, she can give a good account of herself. Possibly adopting a "If you can't beat them, join them" philosophy, Claire now takes a keen interest in football and has become quite knowledgeable about the game though she is not a life-long fan.

She was, in fact, introduced to football at a Pittodrie game to which she was invited by the same mutual friends through whom we had met a short time earlier at a party they gave. To this day, she claims that match as the start of our romance, swearing that she fell in love with my legs.

Born and brought up in Glasgow scarcely more than a mile apart, Claire in Shettleston and myself in Bridgeton, we both had to come to Aberdeen to meet while Claire, a cousin of the Codona family, was working at the Aberdeen beach funfair during the summer.

When Victoria and Mark both passed beyond the baby stage, Claire was able to develop sporting interests in addition to football and she has been attending aerobics classes for the last couple of years in addition to sharing in my business pursuits.

Victoria, too, is keen on football to the extent of liking to kick a ball around the garden, but her main leisure interests at the moment are her piano lessons and the ballet dancing classes which she has been attending for a few years. I have a feeling, however, that she will be quite sports-minded when she is a bit older.

Mark is just beginning to show interest in a ball, but it's a

Is it golf or hockey? A pro-cel-am charity golf tournament at Deeside Golf Club gives me an opportunity to mix with showbiz personalities such as actor Garfield Morgan.

bit early to decide if he has any footballing talent. I'm resolved, however, not to be the kind of father who tries to relive his own youth by moulding his son's sporting career. Mark will get all the encouragement he wants in whatever sport he takes up, but it will be his own choice.

The choice of sports available to youngsters nowadays is so

much wider than it was in my schooldays when, apart from football, athletics was the only outdoor sporting pursuit on offer. I had a go at running and jumping and won the school's intermediate athletics championship – it was a relatively small school which limited the competition in terms of numbers and at that time I was bigger than most boys of my age.

Living in the East End of Glasgow possibly contributed to this restricted choice of sports. I came to realise that only much later when the Dons went to Gordonstoun for pre-season training. Games of cricket and tennis were favoured forms of relaxation, but it was noticeable that the lads who had been brought up in Aberdeen, such as Neale Cooper, Andy Dornan and Neil Simpson, were all better at these sports than the likes of myself, who had never had a cricket bat or tennis racket in my hands during my schooldays.

The older lads at Pittodrie still take delight in relating how Alex Ferguson managed to get me dismissed for a duck in one of these cricket games at Gordonstoun – even though we were both on the same side!

I don't suppose Fergie was any more familiar than I was with the finer points of the game, but, noticing that the Aberdeen lads when batting seemed to have a method in calling for runs, the manager and I decided on our own system. We had an arrangement – or at least I thought we did – that when Fergie hit the ball, it was up to me to decide whether a run was poss-ible. I had just joined the manager at the crease and; before I had faced a ball, Fergie at the other end managed to put bat to ball for what seemed to me a reasonable hit.

"Come on!", I shouted and set off on a run, but halfway down the wicket, I looked up to see Fergie still in his crease, holding up his hand like a policeman halting a line of traffic. Putting on the brakes and going into reverse, I tried to get back to my crease, but was, of course, run out. My displeasure with the failure of our calling system was scarcely improved by the hilarity which the incident provoked – with the laughter led by the manager himself.

I have since made up for the limited scope of my sporting participation by extending my interest in golf, which I find very relaxing after the pressures of professional football. As opposed to a team game, the only pressures in golf are the self-imposed ones. It can, of course, be frustrating at times, but I'm improving, I think, if slowly, and looking forward to lowering my handicap from its present unofficial level of about 18.

As I mentioned earlier, there was no real football background in my family, but when I eventually became absorbed in the game I was given every encouragement by my parents. The extent of this can be gauged by the three-week visit to America I had with the Glasgow Primary Select, a venture which cost my parents some financial sacrifice. At that time I was the oldest of a family of four children with two brothers and a sister, but after my father and mother separated, my mother subsequently remarried and presented us with another sister. My half-sister, Mary Tough, has won international recognition at netball, but neither of my brothers, Brian or Graham, progressed beyond amateur level as footballers.

Following my parents' separation, I kept in touch with my father and up until his death a few years ago, he attended some of the matches when Aberdeen played in the Glasgow area.

Although my parents encouraged my early football interest, they wanted me to stay on at school and complete my education before deciding on a career. For me, however, another year or two at school did not appeal nearly as much as the prospect of playing football as a full-time job. Apart from my preoccupation with football, I was, as I've already explained, anxious to get away to new surroundings. As a kid, I loved living in Glasgow, but in adolescence it became a place to get out of. That was partly because I had changed, but even more because the atmosphere of the east end of the city had changed.

At the time, I had no doubts that I was doing the right thing – and for me it probably was right – but with hindsight I don't know if I would recommend it to a young aspiring professional footballer of today. The system of calling up 'S'-form signings to serve initially as ground staff boys may have its merits in giving the youngster an introduction to the atmosphere of a full-time football club, but if he has any scholarly prospects at all, I think he would be well-advised to remain at school and obtain all the academic qualifications he can, meanwhile confining his football to the minor grades, before plunging into the professional pool.

The trouble is that, to a soccer-mad 16-year-old, the glamour, real or imagined, of full-time football is a strong magnet, and if his parents, as was the case with mine, are not well-versed in what is involved in the early stages of a professional football career, they are not able to give the kind of advice he needs.

In that respect at least, I feel I would be better equipped than my father was at the outset of my soccer career almost 20 years ago to advise Mark if he should ever contemplate following in my footsteps.

CHAPTER TWENTY

The Way Ahead

IN THE course of my 18 years at Pittodrie, I have had a number of opportunities to move to other clubs – and I have given such a move serious consideration on several of these occasions.

A couple of these proposed transfers – involving Sunderland in 1980 and Rangers two years later – were well-publicised at the time, but there were other occasions when the clubs expressing an interest in me were not named publicly, and, indeed, in some instances, even I did not know of the interest until later. I can, however, now reveal that the inquiries included two from abroad in Spanish club Real Betis and a French Second Division outfit.

I mentioned in an earlier chapter that Bristol City were prepared to offer a ten-year contract to attract me to Ashton Gate, but that bid was something of an exception in that it came while I was in mid-contract. The other possibilities of me moving from Pittodrie all arose on the expiry of a contract because I believe firmly that once a contract is signed, it should be honoured in spirit as well as in fact unless both parties want it dissolved. When such a contract expires, however, the player has a duty to his family to secure the best possible deal in his next contract.

The Sunderland offer was, I suppose, the closest I came to leaving Pittodrie in that I actually visited Roker Park for discussions with manager Ken Knighton. I was very impressed by the set-up at Sunderland, who were prepared to pay Aberdeen a £300,000 fee – by 1980 standards a substantial sum. After a lot of thought, however, I felt the move was not right for me and I re-signed for Aberdeen.

I experienced a similar feeling two years later when Rangers were interested in signing me. This time I only got as far as talking to Rangers' manager John Greig on the telephone as there was this time an additional argument against accepting an offer from the Ibrox club. Getting away from a Glasgow environment was, after all, one of the reasons why I had joined Aberdeen in the first place, and although I was 11 years older – and wiser – at the time Rangers wanted me, I still preferred the quality of life I could have in Aberdeen to that of my native city.

As things turned out, the instinctive feelings I had against moves to Sunderland and Rangers were providential in each case. Shortly after I re-signed for Aberdeen in 1980, a group of local businessmen got together and organised a testimonial for me, and the season after I had rejected Rangers saw the Dons win the European Cup-Winners' Cup.

Whenever the possibility of a transfer came up it was, almost invariably, a case of the interested club being prepared to offer me more lucrative terms than Aberdeen's, particularly in the matter of signing-on fees, so it boiled down to weighing purely financial considerations against other factors, principally the strength of the roots which my family and I have put down here in the Granite City and the feelings of stability which playing for the Aberdeen club and living in the city have afforded me.

There are some offers which simply cannot be turned down because they come from one of an élite group of maybe half-a-dozen clubs either in England or on the Continent who are such institutions that signing for them gives a player security for life. None of the bids made for me, however, quite came into this category and I have had no regrets over successive decisions to remain at Pittodrie.

What, then, lies ahead? Well, nothing can be taken for granted when it comes to deciding how long one's football career will last – this was underlined for me last season when for the first time I, who had previously had scant sympathy for victims of long-term injuries, discovered the frustration imposed by a long spell on the sidelines after a knee operation. It was an experience all the more traumatic because of its rarity in my career.

Given reasonable luck, however, I hope to carry on playing until I'm 36, which will be the end of the 1990-91 season, and the completion of my present contract with Aberdeen. I would dearly love to reach that target date, for it would bring my term at Pittodrie to a nice round figure at 20 years. I'm confident that I can maintain my form for at least that length of time, for I would not wish to retain my team place on anything other than merit.

The same applies to my international career. Much as I would love to play in the World Cup finals for a third time when they are staged in Italy next summer, I don't want to be judged either on my past record of over 60 international caps or the fact that I'm 34 years old. All I ask of the national team manager is that he judges me strictly on whether my form is good enough to warrant my selection for the Scotland squad. That has always been my standpoint, and while there have been times when I have not agreed with Scotland managers' decisions in this respect, I appreciate that these are frequently influenced by tactical considerations and his own view of the best combination for a particular match.

Now that I have recovered from last season's operation and have had the benefit of a thorough pre-season build-up, however, I feel that I can make a worthwhile contribution to the cause of both club and country over the next 18 months or so.

When the time does come to hang up my boots, I'll be the first to recognise it. I've always been fairly critical of my own performances and I wouldn't wish to continue playing in the knowledge that the standards I set myself are not being met. Another thing I learned from last season's long lay-off is that you can make physical demands on the body beyond what it is capable of handling only for so long before it rebels.

The decision to pack up playing will be all the easier to make if I have a new challenge to fill the void which would undoubtedly be left in my life, and I have tried to make provision for this by opening up two avenues for further exploration. Last summer I gained my final coaching certificate at the SFA summer school at Largs and I'm now fully qualified for that aspect of football managership, if that is where my future lies. Alternatively, I could devote all my time to developing the business interests I have been working on as an adjunct to my football career in recent years.

Initially this involved me in a partnership which eventually built up to ownership of four public houses, but with my football commitments always given first consideration, it proved

Launching out into the business world. Pittodrie club-mates Eric Black, Jim Leighton, Neil Simpson, Andy Watson and John Hewitt help me open up the bubbly to celebrate the opening of my first business venture in 1983.

an unsatisfactory arrangement, so my partner and I agreed amicably to go our separate ways. Aiming for more flexibility, Claire and I now own one pub, the Parkway at the Bridge of Don, with a manager looking after its day-to-day running and we are also involved with others in a private nursing home project.

While these business interests have always been secondary to my football, the challenge they presented has been very stimulating, even to the extent of destroying a piece of Pittodrie folklore. Over the years I have somehow acquired a reputation for being able to sleep anywhere, anytime, and I must admit that in the past it was not unknown for me to come home from training at lunchtime, stretch out on the couch and sleep most of the afternoon. Nowadays, however, between football and business affairs, I'm kept on the go all day, I haven't time to sleep during daylight hours, and I don't think I'll ever be able to return to my former habits.

As I've said, playing football remains my number one interest and that is why I think football management would be given preference to business if a suitable opportunity were to present itself when I decide to stop playing. I have been involved in professional football so long now that cutting myself off from it completely when I hang up my boots would, I feel, leave too much of a gap in my life, one which a move into management would help fill.

Many people seem to have been expecting me to make such a move before now. My name was being bandied about in various combinations with others in the speculation 18 months ago over who would fill the Aberdeen vacancy following the departure of Ian Porterfield. During that period of uncertainty I gave no indication to the Aberdeen board of any interest in the managership because I wanted to continue as a player. I know some of the speculation suggested a player-manager arrangement, but it seems to me that the experience of Kenny Dalglish and Graeme Souness has shown that to be essentially a short-term thing. Sooner rather than later the managerial responsibilities overtake the playing opportunities.

Do I have the right qualities to make a good manager? Well, in all due modesty, I obviously think so, otherwise I wouldn't be contemplating managership as a future option, although I would be the first to agree that a good player doesn't always make a good manager.

I might not be prepared to sacrifice everything for the sake of the job as some managers do. For someone like Alex Ferguson, for instance, whose passion for football is all-consuming, everything else is secondary. I don't think that would be so in my case, but anything I go into receives my 100% attention and I love football too much to give it anything less.

As for the practicalities of the job, I feel my association over the years with some of the best football managers in the business has taught me a lot about the many different aspects of managership, such as getting the best out of players, satisfying the sometimes differing demands of the club directors on one hand and the supporters on the other, and handling the media.

The experience I have gained outside football in recent years in pursuing my business interests could also prove useful to me in soccer management, particularly in the area of dealing with people, whether they be players, directors, supporters or Pressmen. These interests, incidentally, have enabled me to take a more detached view of the world of professional football which has been my whole life for so long. One of the things I have come to realise through looking after myself in the business world is that the average full-time footballer does not appreciate how cosseted he is in everyday matters, such as having all his travel arrangements and his accommodation bookings made for him.

During my injury absence last season, for example, I was travelling independently to one of the games, having arranged to meet the squad at the hotel where we usually have lunch before the game. It was only when I was in the car that I realised that although I had been to that hotel countless times, I wasn't too sure how to get there because I was so accustomed to being delivered right to the entrance by the team bus and picked up again after lunch.

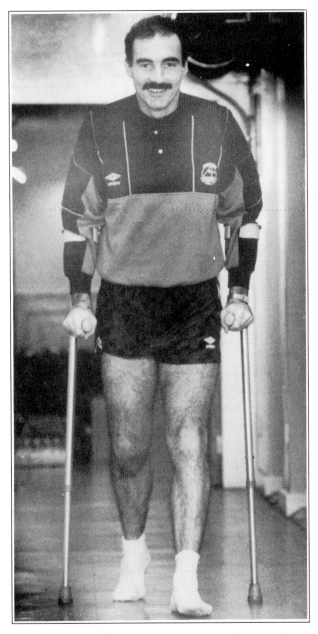

Starting the fight back to fitness after my knee operation.

Yes, entering the world of business has certainly broadened my horizons as well as giving me extra security in preparation for the time when my playing career ends, but I rather think that when that day arrives, it would be too great a wrench to depart from the football scene altogether. Going into the managerial side would maintain my connections with the game as well as providing the sort of fresh challenge I would welcome, and, at the moment, that seems the likelier avenue for me to take, even though it may entail pulling up my Aberdeen roots.

Time will tell!

MILESTONES

2 May 1955 – Born

June 1969 – Signed for Aberdeen as a 14-year-old striker.

July 1971 – Called up for Pittodrie and farmed out to Peterhead, finishing as club's leading scorer for season 1971-72 with 23 goals and helping club win the Aberdeenshire Cup.

16 December 1972 – Played as central defender for first time in Reserve League game v Rangers 'A' at Pittodrie.

28 April 1973 – Made competitive first-team debut against Morton at Cappielow. Substituted for Arthur Graham and played as striker.

19 September 1973 – European debut in UEFA Cup first-round tie against Finn Harps (Eire) at Pittodrie.

13 March 1974 – First Under-23 cap (at right-back) against England at St James' Park, Newcastle.

15 March 1975 – 100th first-team appearance for Aberdeen against Partick Thistle at Firhill.

June 1 1975 – Full international debut (in midfield) against Rumania in Bucharest.

24 November 1975 – Married Claire

4 December 1975 – Appointed Dons' captain in succession to Bobby Clark.

6 November 1976 – Led Aberdeen to League Cup victory over Celtic (after extra time).

26 February 1977 – 200th first-team appearance for Aberdeen in Scottish Cup fourth-round tie against Dundee at Dens Park.

11 November 1978 – 300th first-team appearance for Aberdeen against Motherwell at Fir Park.

7 May 1980 – Led Aberdeen to first League Championship title-win since 1955.

21 May 1980 – Scored Scotland's only goal in 1-0 Home Championship win over Wales at Hampden Park.

13 June 1980 – Daughter Victoria born

30 August 1980 – 400th first-team appearance for Aberdeen in second leg of League Cup-tie against Berwick Rangers at Shielfield Park.

16 August 1981 – Testimonial match Aberdeen v Tottenham

17 April 1982 – 500th first-team appearance for Aberdeen against Morton at Cappielow.

22 May 1982 – Led Aberdeen to first of three successive Scottish Cup triumphs.

18 June 1982 – Won 18th Scotland cap v Brazil in World Cup finals in Spain, beating Bobby Clark's club record for full caps.

1 September 1982 – Scored first European goal in second leg of Cup-Winners' Cup preliminary-round tie against FC Sion in Switzerland.

11 May 1983 – Led Aberdeen to European Cup-Winners' Cup final victory over Real Madrid (after extra time) in Gothenburg.

12 June 1983 – Captained Scotland for first time during Canadian tour.

2 November 1983 – 600th first-team appearance for Aberdeen in second leg of Cup-Winners' Cup second-round tie against Beveren at Pittodrie.

20 December 1983 – Led Aberdeen to European Super Cup victory over SV Hamburg.

May 1984 – Voted "Player of the Year" by both Scottish Football Writers' Association and Scottish Professional Footballers' Association.

18 June 1984 – Son Mark born

10 August 1985 – 700th first-team appearance for Aberdeen against Hibs at Pittodrie, passing Bobby Clark's club record of 697.

5 March 1986 – 50th European appearance in first leg of European Cup quarter-final against IFK Gothenburg at Pittodrie. Scored second European goal in 2-2 draw.

8 June 1986 – 50th full cap against West Germany in World Cup finals in Mexico.

17 May 1988 – 60th full cap against Colombia in Rous Cup game at Hampden.

Willie Miller's Appearances for Aberdeen

Season	League	League Cup	Scottish Cup	EURO Super Cup	EURO Champ Cup	ECWC	UEFA Cup	Texaco A/S Cup	Dryboro' Cup	A'shire Cup	Friendly	Total
1972-73	1(1s)										2(2s)	3(3s)
1973-74	31	9	1				4				10(1s)	55(1s)
1974-75	34	6	4					2			2	48
1975-76	36	6	2					4			8	56
1976-77	36	8	3					4			3	54
1977-78	36	6	6				2				6	56
1978-79	34	8	5			4					9	60
1979-80	31	8	5				2				8(1s)	55(1s)
1980-81	33	6	1		4				1		7	56
1981-82	36	10	6				6		3	2	8	66
1982-83	36	8	5			11					2	62
1983-84	34	9	7	2		8					10	70
1984-85	34	1	6		2						9	52
1985-86	33	6	6		6						7	58
1986-87	36	2	3			2					4	47
1987-88	42	5	6				4				2	59
1988-89	21	5	–				2				5	33
TOTALS	544(1s)	103	66	2	12	25	20	10	4	2	102(4s)	890(5s)